T0408854

塩

豚骨

醤油

味噌

MISO RAMEN-SHOYU RAMEN-TONKOTSU RAMEN-SHIO RAMEN

ラ・カロパーの本 A book by Deborah Kaloper デボラ・カロパーの本

マン・ゾル Photography by Daniel Herrmann-Zoll 写真撮影・ダ

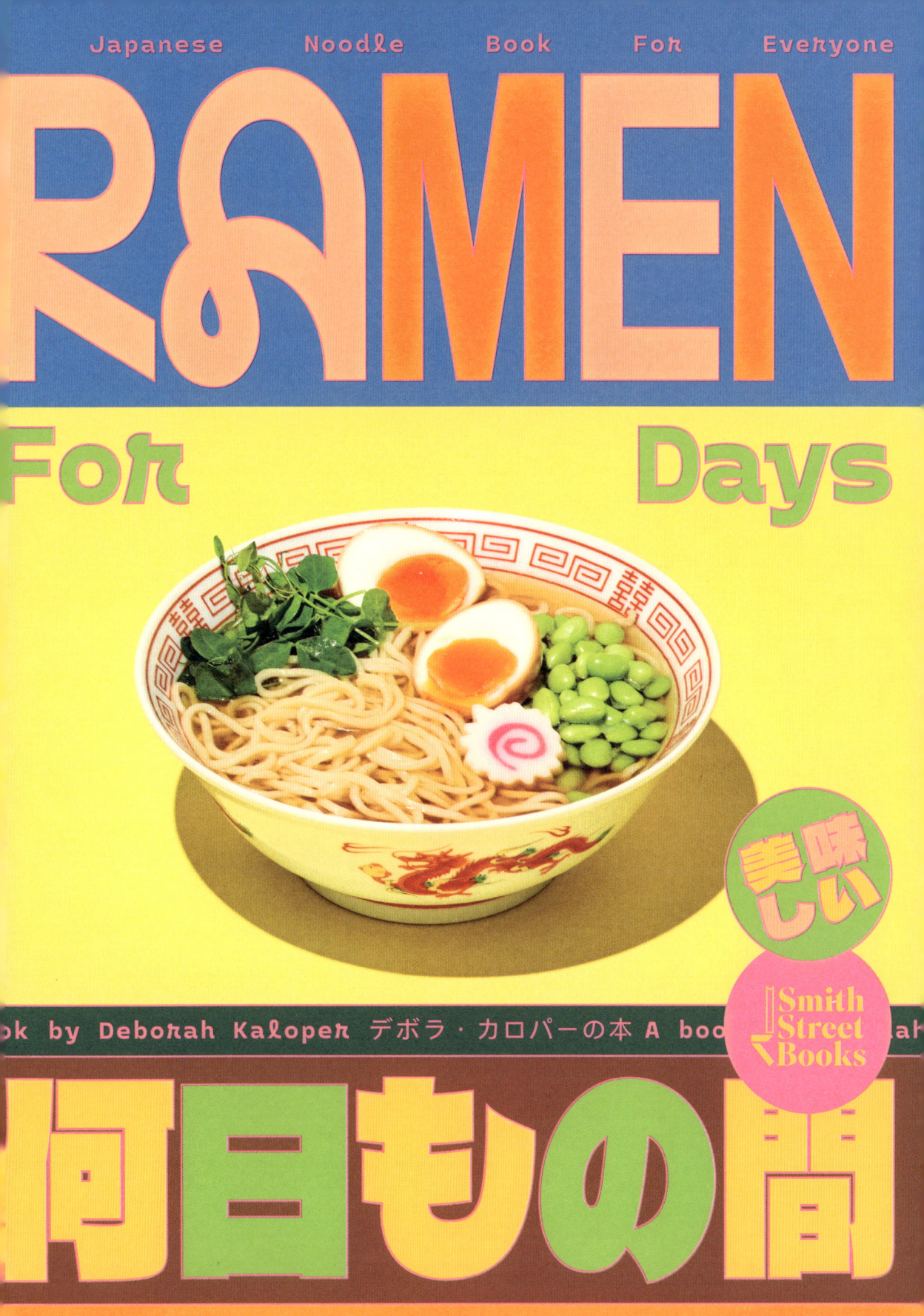

Japanese Noodle Book For Everyone

RAMEN

For Days

美味しい

Smith Street Books

...ok by Deborah Kaloper デボラ・カロパーの本 A boo... ...ah...

何日もの間

ハーマン・ゾル Photography by Daniel Herrmann-Zoll 写真撮影

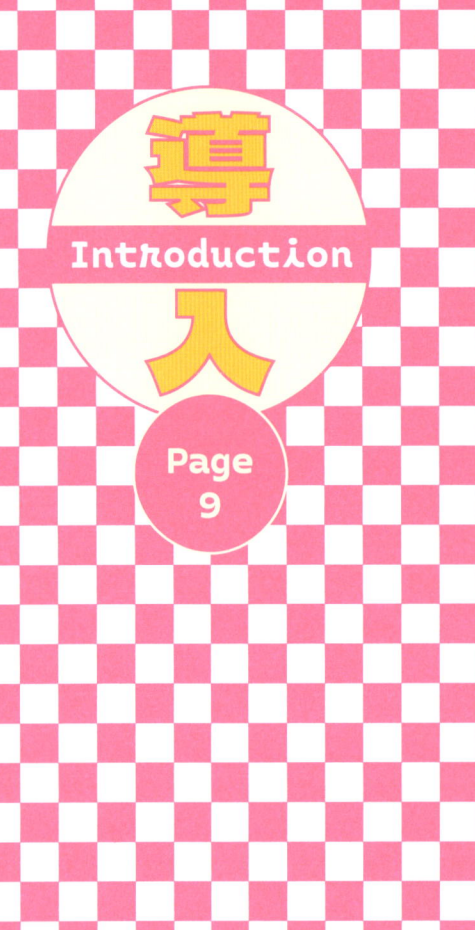

導入

Introduction

Page 9

ESSENTIALS

必需品

Page 12

Bean Sprouts
Black Garlic Oil
Chilli Oil
Corn
Garlic Chives
Ginger
Kabocha
Katsuobushi
Kimchi
Menma
Mirin
Miso
Mushrooms
Noodles
Ponzu
Radish
Rice Vinegar
Sake
Seaweeds
Sesame Seeds
Shichimi Togarashi

BASICS

Miso Broth	23
Shoyu Broth	25
Tonkotsu Broth	27
Shio Broth	29
Vegan Broth	31
Dashi Stock	33
Vegan Dashi Stock	33
Ramen Noodles	37

TOPPINGS and EXTRAS

Seasoned Eggs	44
Hot Springs Eggs	44
Umami Mushroom Powder	45
Black Garlic Oil	45
Chashu Pork	46
Shredded Pork Shoulder	47
Braised Pork Belly	48
Japanese Quick Pickles	49
Gyozas	50
Vegetable Gyozas	52
Seafood Gyozas	53
Pork Gyozas	53
Fish Cakes	57
Kimchi	58
Garlic Chips	60
Wakame Sesame Salt	60
Furikake	61
Pickled Shiitake Mushrooms	61
Rendered Pork Fat	62
Sweet Braised Kombu	62
Miso Butter Bombs	63
Seaweed Butter Bombs	63

MiSO
RAMEN 64

67
BUTTERED CORN, BACON AND AJITSUKE TAMAGO RAMEN

69
SPICY PRAWN, CHASHU PORK AND ENOKI MUSHROOM RAMEN

71
SEAFOOD RAMEN

Shoyu
RAMEN 80

83
PORK KARAAGE RAMEN

85
WAGYU RAMEN

87
BEAN CURD, ZUCCHINI AND KIMCHI VEGAN RAMEN

Tonkotsu
RAMEN 96

99
CHICKEN KARAAGE RAMEN

101
PORK SHOULDER, ONSEN TAMAGO AND NARUTOMAKI RAMEN

103
CHASHU, AJITSUKE TAMAGO AND MENMA RAMEN

Shio
RAMEN 112

115
SEARED SCALLOPS, BUTTERED CORN AND LEEK RAMEN

117
PANKO CHICKEN RAMEN

119
SPINACH, BOK CHOY AND EDAMAME RAMEN

73

CHASHU PORK, CABBAGE
AND BEAN SPROUT RAMEN

75

BARBECUE
CHICKEN RAMEN

77

KAKUNI
RAMEN

79

SMOKED TOFU, MISO-GLAZED
CARROTS AND EGGPLANT RAMEN

89

SEAFOOD GYOZA AND
CHASHU RAMEN

91

MUSHROOM
RAMEN

93

SEAFOOD GYOZA AND
GRILLED PRAWN RAMEN

95

KAKUNI, VEGETABLE GYOZA
AND QUAIL EGG RAMEN

105

CHASHU PORK AND KING
OYSTER MUSHROOM RAMEN

107

SPICY MINCED
PORK RAMEN

109

PORK GYOZA AND BUTTERED
CABBAGE RAMEN

111

SALT AND PEPPER
TOFU RAMEN

121

SQUID INK
RAMEN

123

KAKUNI, FRIED EGG AND
SPRING ONION RAMEN

125

VEGETABLE GYOZA, KABOCHA
AND SHIITAKE RAMEN

127

MINCED CHICKEN WITH
SPICY BEAN PASTE RAMEN

Ramen may have started out as an unassuming and nourishing quick factory worker's meal, but it has evolved. This simple bowl of noodles and broth has been elevated to the status of Japanese cultural icon that now carries a worldwide cult following.

Although history shows that in the 1890s a Chinese-influenced noodle soup (chanpon) made with pork and vegetables was being served in a Nagasaki restaurant, many prefer a different story for the beginning of ramen. The folklore goes something like this: in 1955 on the island of Hokkaido, a factory worker was eating his bowl of miso soup in a Sapporo bar. Still hungry, he asked to have noodles put in his soup, and so miso ramen was born. He started a trend that became a national movement revolving around a few humble ingredients: broth, noodles, meat and vegetables. Soon, other regions and cities picked up the trend, and various styles of ramen developed and evolved according to regional ingredients and palates. The appetite for ramen noodles grew further when, in 1958, Mr Momofuku Ando of the Nissin Food Products Company commercialised the production of instant ramen noodles, making them available to everyone. As a result, by the 1970s, the world was eating 'cup noodles' and thinking of them as ramen.

This is a far cry from the elevated status of ramen today where noodle-making techniques are studied, stocks and broths are painstakingly and lovingly conjured and ingredient ideas are pushed beyond simple pork belly or chashu.

Hungry patrons wait in long lines that coil around restaurant buildings, queueing for hours just to get a seat at the bar, where ramen chefs have become ramen masters, possessing the status of rock stars.

The anatomy of a ramen bowl is simple and complex at the same time. It is a matrix of flavours and textures, a crescendo of sensational aromas, wafting together in harmony. At its heart lie the noodles. They may be thin or thick, curly or straight, but they must be firm and springy to the bite and be able to withstand the heat of the broth without becoming soggy. Kansui, known as lye water or alkaline water, is made using alkaline salts, and it is this ingredient that gives the noodles their distinctive yellow hue and their texture.

Then there's the broth, with its complex layers of umami flavour. There are four basic styles: shio, which is a salty broth, often made using chicken and fish as a flavour base; tonkotsu, a thick, collagen-rich, fatty pork broth, made by boiling pork bones for up to 48 hours; shoyu, which uses soy sauce as its main flavour component and chicken, vegetables and sometimes beef as its stock base; and miso broth, which, as the name suggests, uses copious amounts of miso paste and often uses a chicken, fish and pork fat base. Within all these broths is the tare, the 'mind' of the soup: a seasoning concoction that delivers the umami layers needed to create an overall balanced taste. The tare may include soy sauce, sake, mirin, salt, garlic, pork fat, dashi and even ground sesame seeds. Each tare is unique to the broth, to the ramen shop and to the region.

The body of the ramen is in the toppings. Classics such as chashu, menma, ajitsuke tamago and nori have stood the test of time, but ramen makers are becoming more adventurous. Now, almost anything goes, allowing you to create your own flavour combinations in every bowl.

So start cooking and be adventurous. Experiment with toppings and tares and find your own way through this delicious bowl of comfort food, one slurp at a time.

In the words of Momofuku Ando: 'Peace will come to the world when people have enough (noodles) to eat.'

1
BEAN SPROUTS

Both mung beans and soy beans are commonly sprouted. Bean sprouts are used in Asian dishes to add a fresh, crisp and crunchy texture.

2
BLACK GARLIC OIL

A burnt garlic and sesame oil, black garlic oil creates an added layer of savoury richness when drizzled over ramen dishes.

3
CHILLI OIL

Chilli-infused oil, or rayu, is a condiment commonly used for kicking up the heat and spice levels in Japanese cuisine. Made with toasted sesame oil, corn oil or a blend of oils, this spicy hot oil is a pantry staple. Drizzled across steaming ramen, the oil beads on the broth surface, ensuring that every noodle it touches has some fiery flavour attached.

4
CORN

Sweetcorn started appearing atop ramen in Hokkaido, Japan's northernmost island, over 25 years ago, where it is farmed along with other staples such as wheat and soy beans. Freshly shucked corn kernels add a sweet and crunchy element to ramen and can be topped with a knob of butter or a butter bomb.

5
GARLIC CHIVES

Known as *nira* in Japan, freshly chopped garlic chives make a great addition to ramen, imparting a herbaceous note, somewhere between garlic and spring onion (scallion). Their blossoms are edible and can also be sprinkled on top of ramen.

6
GINGER

Fresh ginger adds a punch of heat to warm up any dish and is commonly used in Japanese noodle dishes, soups and marinades.

Beni shoga is julienned ginger that has been pickled in plum vinegar with purple shiso leaves to turn it red. It is equally perfect served with a fatty, rich pork ramen or a simple vegetable ramen to cleanse and lift the flavours.

7
KABOCHA

This Japanese pumpkin is also known as Japanese winter squash. Sweet in flavour, this dense, orange-fleshed vegetable can be steamed, grilled (broiled) or roasted before being added to ramen.

8
KATSUOBUSHI

Also known as dried bonito flakes, katsuobushi is an essential ingredient in dashi. Paper-thin shavings of dried smoked bonito, resembling fine wood shavings, deliver a unique yet ubiquitous flavour quintessential to Japanese cooking. Added to soups, stocks and broths or simply used in small amounts as a flavouring garnish, it lends a seriously layered umami-rich hit.

必需品

9
KIMCHI

Korean in origin, this spicy dish has crossed many continents and cultures. Made from fermented cabbage, daikon, onion, ginger and lots of chilli powder and garlic, kimchi has a pungent smell and a distinct flavour that is very moreish and has accrued fans worldwide. It's simple to make; add it to your ramen pantry and you won't be disappointed.

10
MENMA

For many, this Japanese condiment is an acquired taste, yet menma is a 'classic' topping in the world of ramen. It is made from lactate-fermented bamboo shoots and is available in most Asian supermarkets.

11
MIRIN

A Japanese sweet rice wine with a delicate, subtle flavour, mirin is often used in cooking to marinate meats and fish, masking their strong flavours, and to create shiny glazed sauces, providing an overall balance to many dishes.

12
MISO

This fermented soy bean paste is commonly made from a combination of soy beans and grains, such as rice or barley, and is fermented with koji – a yeast used in the production of sake and mirin. There are many varieties of miso paste, all with unique flavours and specific culinary uses. The ingredients it is made with and the length of the ferment time determine its final colour and flavour. Two of the most common miso pastes are shiro miso, a young, sweet, white miso paste made from rice, most often used to marinate vegetables and fish, and for adding to mild-flavoured soups; and aka miso, a reddish-brown miso paste, which is fermented for longer and usually made with barley. It has a rich, salty, intense umami taste and is used for bold-flavoured soups, stews and meats.

13
MUSHROOMS

Dried or fresh, a wide variety of mushrooms are used to flavour ramen. Dried shiitakes give vegan dashi or soup stock a powerful umami lift, while fresh shiitakes, more delicate in flavour, give a chewy, brawny quality to dishes. Enoki, also known as *enokitake* or *enokidake*, are fragile, long, thin, white mushrooms. They are used in soups, salads and stir-fries and have a soft, mild flavour. Wood ear, also known as black fungus or cloud ear mushrooms, are available fresh but are commonly used rehydrated from dried. Subtle in flavour, they have a firm, gelatinous texture. King brown mushrooms are part of the oyster mushroom family. Rich in flavour and firm in texture, they are used in sautés and perfect stir-fried and served in ramen.

14
NOODLES

Ramen noodles are made with wheat flour, water and kansui, an alkaline mineral powder that gives them a yellowish hue and springy bite. Thick or thin, curly or straight, there is a noodle to suit every type of ramen. If you are gluten intolerant, you can substitute rice or kelp noodles.

15
PONZU

Ponzu is a blend of soy sauce and yuzu juice. Yuzu is a citrus fruit with a mild tang and a lemon–orange flavour. Ponzu is used in marinades, dressings and fish dishes.

16
RADISH

Daikon is a Japanese white radish with a mild peppery taste. It can be eaten raw, cooked or pickled and used in salads and soups and to accompany fatty meat dishes, such as pork. Serve pickled alongside a rich pork ramen.

17
RICE VINEGAR

A mild and mellow vinegar made from brown or white rice, this is a foundation in Japanese cooking. Use it to make pickles and dressings.

18
SAKE

Sake is a Japanese rice wine and one of the 'holy trinity' of essential ingredients in Japanese cooking, along with soy sauce and mirin. Cooking sake has a lower alcohol content than drinking sake and is less sweet than mirin. Use in marinades, sauces and tares.

19
SEAWEEDS

Seaweeds or sea vegetables are rich in vitamins and minerals. They play an ever-present role in Japanese cooking and in the world of ramen. Kombu, also known as kelp or *konbu*, is deep green in colour and has a large, wide, flat shape. Indispensable in the making of dashi, it can be used in many stocks, stews and condiments, adding a rich umami flavour that delivers a salty seawater essence. Nori, also known as *laver*, is most commonly used in sushi-making but has a deserved place in the ramen bowl. Processed into toasted flat sheets, cut into squares and perched inside the bowl, or crumbled and sprinkled on top, it enhances every dish with its mineral-rich flavour. Wakame is soft in texture, mild and almost sweet in flavour and is most commonly used in miso soup. Available dried in long strips or shredded into small pieces, it easily rehydrates for a quick addition to your ramen of choice.

20
SESAME SEEDS

Black and white sesame seeds are different varieties from the same plant. Black sesame seeds are unhulled and have a slightly nuttier, more robust taste than white sesame seeds, which have been hulled. Both can be toasted to release their aromatic buttery flavour. Used as a garnish for ramen, ground up as tahini for tonkotsu or in a condiment, such as gomasio, these little seeds are highly versatile.

21
SHICHIMI TOGARASHI

Also known as *nana iro togarashi*, this Japanese spice mix has been used for hundreds of years to season soups, noodles and rice dishes. It is a blend of ground dried red chilli, sansho chilli, black and white sesame seeds, orange zest, seaweed and ginger. Sprinkle over your ramen toppings.

必需品 ESSENTIALS

Miso Broth

Makes enough for 2 bowls of ramen

800 ml (27 fl oz) Chicken, Pork and Vegetable Stock (see below)	
1 × quantity Miso Tare (see below)	
2 teaspoons Rendered Pork Fat or chicken fat	P.62

Chicken, Pork and Vegetable Stock (Makes 2 litres / 8 cups)

1 kg (2 lb 3 oz) chicken wings

1 kg (2 lb 3 oz) chicken necks

1 kg (2 lb 3 oz) pork bones, fatty ribs or trotters, sawn into quarters by your butcher

2 onions, quartered

1 carrot, quartered

1 leek, quartered

4 dried shiitake mushrooms

6 garlic cloves, smashed

1 teaspoon black peppercorns

30 g (1 oz) ginger, chopped

Miso Tare

100 g (⅓ cup) white miso paste

100 g (⅓ cup) red miso paste

3 garlic cloves, finely grated

2 teaspoons mirin

1 teaspoon toasted sesame oil

pinch of ground white pepper

1 teaspoon tahini (optional)

(STOCK) Place the chicken wings and necks and pork bones, ribs or trotters in a large stockpot. Cover with water and bring to the boil. Blanch for 10–15 minutes, then drain, discarding the liquid.

Rinse and scrub the bones of any scum, transfer to a clean stockpot and add the remaining ingredients. Cover with 4.5 litres (4¾ quarts) water, bring to the boil and skim off any impurities that rise to the surface. Reduce the heat, cover and simmer for 2–2½ hours, until you are left with about 2 litres (8 cups) of liquid.

Strain the stock and discard the solids. Leave to cool before refrigerating. The stock will keep in an airtight container in the fridge for up to 5 days, or in the freezer for up to 3 months.

(TARE) Whisk the ingredients in a small bowl to combine. The tare will keep in an airtight container in the fridge for up to 5 days.

(BROTH) In a small saucepan, bring the stock to a rapid simmer. Whisk in the miso tare and add the pork or chicken fat.

Serve over ramen noodles with your favourite toppings.

基本 **BASICS**

Shoyu Broth

Makes enough for 2 bowls of ramen
800 ml (27 fl oz) Chicken, Vegetable and Fish Stock (see below)
1 × quantity Shoyu Tare (see below)
1½ tablespoons Rendered Pork Fat or chicken fat P.62

Chicken, Vegetable and Fish Stock (Makes 2 litres / 8 cups)
1 kg (2 lb 3 oz) chicken wings
1 kg (2 lb 3 oz) chicken necks
2 onions, quartered
1 carrot, quartered
1 leek, quartered
4 dried shiitake mushrooms
6 garlic cloves, smashed
1 teaspoon black peppercorns
15 g (½ oz) bonito flakes (katsuobushi)

Shoyu Tare
70 ml (2¼ fl oz) soy sauce
3 teaspoons Dashi Stock P.33
1½ teaspoons sake
1½ teaspoons mirin
1½ teaspoons toasted sesame oil
¼ teaspoon finely grated ginger
⅓ teaspoon finely grated garlic

(STOCK) Place the chicken wings and necks, vegetables, garlic and peppercorns in a large stockpot and cover with 5 litres (5¼ quarts) water. Bring to the boil and skim off any impurities that rise to the surface. Reduce the heat, cover and simmer for 2–2½ hours, until you are left with about 2 litres (8 cups) of stock. Add the bonito flakes, simmer for 5 minutes, then remove from the heat.

Strain the stock and discard the solids.

Leave to cool before refrigerating. The stock will keep in an airtight container in the fridge for up to 5 days or in the freezer for up to 3 months.

(TARE) Whisk the ingredients in a small bowl to combine. The tare will keep in an airtight container in the fridge for up to 1 week.

(BROTH) Combine all the ingredients in a saucepan and bring to a simmer, whisking.

Serve over ramen noodles with your favourite toppings.

Tonkotsu Broth

Makes enough for 2 bowls of ramen

800 ml (27 fl oz) Tonkotsu Stock (see below)	
1 × quantity Tonkotsu Tare (see below)	
1½ tablespoons Rendered Pork Fat	P.62

Tonkotsu Stock (Makes 2 litres / 8 cups)

2 kg (4 lb 6 oz) pork thigh bones, sawn into 3 cm (1¼ in) discs by your butcher

2 pig's trotters, sawn in half by your butcher

1 onion, quartered

8 garlic cloves, smashed

Tonkotsu Tare

2 tablespoons Rendered Pork Fat	P.62
1½ tablespoons tahini	
2 teaspoons soy sauce or chashu braising liquid	P.46
1 teaspoon mirin	
1½ teaspoons sea salt	
⅛ teaspoon ground white pepper	
2 garlic cloves, finely grated	

(STOCK) Place the bones and trotters in a large stockpot and cover with water. Bring to the boil and blanch for 10–15 minutes, then drain, discarding the liquid. Rinse and scrub the bones and trotters, removing any brown-coloured bits of blood as they will discolour the broth.

Return the bones and trotters to a clean stockpot, add 6 litres (6⅓ quarts) water and bring to the boil. Skim off any impurities that rise to the surface, then cover and boil rapidly for 6 hours, topping up with extra water as needed.

Add the onion and garlic and continue to boil, covered, for a further 2–3 hours, topping up with water. Continue to cook until the liquid has reduced to about 2 litres (8 cups). You should be left with a milky-white, collagen-rich, thick stock.

Strain the broth and discard the bones and vegetables.

Leave the stock to cool before refrigerating. It will keep in an airtight container in the fridge for up to 5 days, or in the freezer for up to 3 months.

(TARE) Whisk the ingredients in a small bowl to combine. The tare will keep in an airtight container in the fridge for up to 5 days.

(BROTH) Combine all the ingredients in a saucepan and bring to a simmer, whisking.

Serve over ramen noodles with your favourite toppings.

基本 BASICS

Shio Broth

Makes enough for 2 bowls of ramen

400 ml (13½ fl oz) Simple Chicken Stock (see below)

400 ml (13½ fl oz) Dashi Stock — P.33

1 × quantity Shio Tare (see below)

1½ tablespoons Rendered Pork Fat or chicken fat — P.62

Simple Chicken Stock (Makes 2 litres / 8 cups)

1 × 2 kg (4 lb 6 oz) organic whole chicken, rinsed

6 garlic cloves, smashed

½ teaspoon white peppercorns

Shio Tare

2 tablespoons fine sea salt

1 tablespoon boiling water

2 tablespoons sake

1 tablespoon mirin

2 teaspoons toasted sesame oil

1 teaspoon soy sauce

1 garlic clove, finely grated

(STOCK) Place the chicken in a large stockpot, cover with 5 litres (5¼ quarts) water and slowly bring to the boil. Skim off any impurities that rise to the surface, then reduce the heat and maintain a slow simmer for about 4 hours, adding the garlic cloves and pepper in the final hour of cooking. You will be left with about 2 litres (8 cups) of stock.

Strain the stock and pick the meat from the bones, reserving it to use in your ramen of choice or in soups or salads.

Leave the stock to cool before refrigerating. It will keep in an airtight container in the fridge for up to 5 days, or in the freezer for up to 3 months. If not using rendered pork fat, skim off the fat that solidifies on the surface of the stock and add it to your shio broth.

(TARE) Place the salt in a bowl, pour the boiling water over and whisk until dissolved. Add the remaining ingredients and whisk to combine. The tare will keep in an airtight container in the fridge for up to 5 days.

(BROTH) Combine all the ingredients in a saucepan and bring to a simmer, whisking.

Serve over ramen noodles with your favourite toppings.

Vegan Broth

Makes enough for 2 bowls of ramen
800 ml (27 fl oz) Vegan Stock (see below)
1 × quantity Vegan Tare (see below)

Vegan Stock (Makes 2 litres / 8 cups)
1 leek, roughly chopped
2 onions, quartered
2 carrots, roughly chopped
4 spring onions (scallions)
3 teaspoons peanut oil
6 dried shiitake mushrooms
6 garlic cloves, smashed
20 g (¾ oz) ginger, chopped
½ teaspoon white peppercorns
15 g (½ oz) kombu

Vegan Tare
100 g (⅓ cup) red miso paste
2 tablespoons tahini
1 tablespoon soy sauce
1 tablespoon mirin
1 tablespoon sake
1 tablespoon ponzu
2 teaspoons toasted sesame oil
1 garlic clove, finely grated
½ teaspoon finely grated ginger

(STOCK) Rinse the leek to remove any grit. Transfer to a bowl, along with the onion, carrot, spring onions and oil. Toss well to combine.

Transfer to a large saucepan over medium–high heat and slightly char the vegetables to deepen their flavour. Add the mushrooms, garlic, ginger and peppercorns, cover with 4 litres (4¼ quarts) water and bring to the boil. Reduce to a rapid simmer and cook for 1–1½ hours, until reduced to about 2 litres (8 cups) of stock. Add the kombu and simmer for 5 minutes, then remove from the heat and leave to infuse in the stock for 15–20 minutes.

Strain the stock, reserving the mushrooms to make Pickled Shiitake Mushrooms (page 61), and reserving the kombu to make Tsukudani (page 62), if you like. Discard the remaining solids.

Leave to cool before refrigerating. The stock will keep in an airtight container in the fridge for up to 5 days, or in the freezer for up to 3 months.

(TARE) Whisk the ingredients in a small bowl to combine. The tare will keep in an airtight container in the fridge for up to 5 days.

(BROTH) Combine the ingredients in a small saucepan and bring to a simmer.

Serve over ramen, rice or kelp noodles with your favourite toppings.

Dashi Stock

Makes 1 litre (4 cups)

15 g (½ oz) kombu

15 g (½ oz) bonito flakes (katsuobushi)

Place the kombu in a large bowl, cover with 1 litre (4 cups) water and set aside in the fridge for 2–3 hours or overnight.

Transfer the liquid to a saucepan and gently heat to 80°C (175°F) – this should take at least 20 minutes.

Simmer at this temperature for 5 minutes, then add the bonito flakes and steep for 5 minutes, keeping the temperature at 80°C. Remove from the heat, strain the liquid and discard the solids.

Leave the stock to cool before refrigerating. It will keep in an airtight container in the fridge for up to 5 days.

Vegan Dashi Stock

Makes 1 litre (4 cups)

15 g (½ oz) kombu

5–6 dried shiitake mushrooms

Place the kombu and mushrooms in a large bowl, cover with 1 litre (4 cups) water and set aside in the fridge for 2–3 hours or overnight.

Transfer the liquid to a saucepan and gently heat to 80°C (175°F) – this should take at least 20 minutes.

Simmer at this temperature for 5 minutes, then steep for 5 minutes, keeping the temperature at 80°C. Remove from the heat and strain the liquid. Keep the kombu for making Tsukudani (page 62), and reserve the shiitakes for your ramen or to make Pickled Shiitake Mushrooms (page 61), if desired.

Leave the stock to cool before refrigerating. It will keep in an airtight container in the fridge for up to 5 days.

基本 **BASICS**

Ramen may be Japan's national dish, but it traces its origins to China. The noodle soup was introduced to Japan by Chinese immigrants in the late 19th or early 20th century and gained popularity thanks to the availability of cheap wheat flour and the rise of instant ramen from the 1950s. Whether thick and wavy or thin and straight, noodles are tailored to suit the broth of each regional variety.

NOODLES

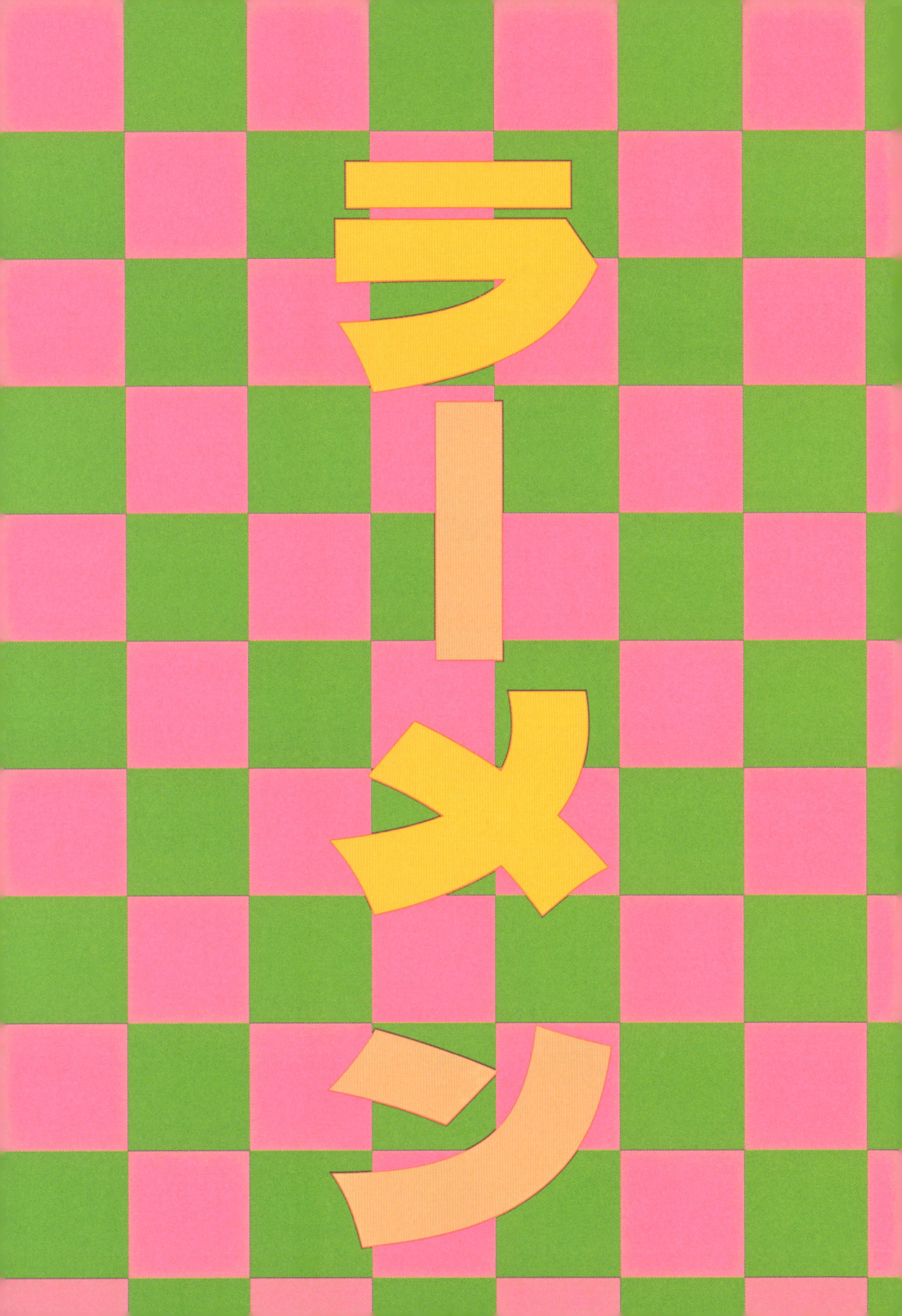

Ramen Noodles

Makes 6 × 120 g (4½ oz) portions

1 teaspoon kansui (sodium carbonate powder; see note)

1 teaspoon fine sea salt

500 g (1 lb 2 oz) 00 flour, plus extra for dusting

Dissolve the kansui and salt in 220 ml (7½ fl oz) water at room temperature.

Place the flour in an electric mixer with a dough hook attachment and mix on low speed while slowly adding the water solution. Mix for 9–10 minutes, increasing the speed slightly towards the end, until you have a very crumbly, pebble-like dough. Depending on your flour, you may need to add up to 3 tablespoons of additional water to reach the desired consistency.

Transfer to a kitchen bench lightly dusted with flour and knead for 2–3 minutes. Bring the dough together and shape into a flat disc. Cover with plastic wrap and set aside in the fridge for 30–40 minutes to soften.

Lightly dust the kitchen bench with flour. Cut the dough into six evenly sized pieces. Working with one piece of dough at a time, and keeping the rest covered, roll the dough through a pasta machine on its widest setting. Fold the dough on top of itself so that it's a double layer and pass through the rollers again.

Reduce the width of the rollers to their next setting and roll the dough through. Fold the dough onto itself again and pass through the machine a second time. Repeat this process again on the third-widest setting, then continue to pass through the machine reducing the width settings, but without folding the dough onto itself.

For thicker noodles, roll the dough until it is 2 mm (⅛ in) thick, then cut into noodles with the spaghetti attachment. For thin noodles, roll the dough until it is 1.5 mm (1/16 in) thick, then cut into noodles with the capellini attachment.

Cook the noodles in a large saucepan of boiling salted water for 45–55 seconds. Drain well, shaking off the excess water, then transfer to serving bowls. Top with your broth and toppings of choice, then slurp away!

The noodles should be eaten the same day they are made.

(NOTE) Kansui is an alkaline powder that gives the noodles their light yellowish colour and chewy texture. It can be found in Asian supermarkets.

Topp

トッピン

and

味付け卵
Ajitsuke Tamago
SEASONED EGGS

温泉卵
Onsen Tamago
HOT SPRINGS EGGS

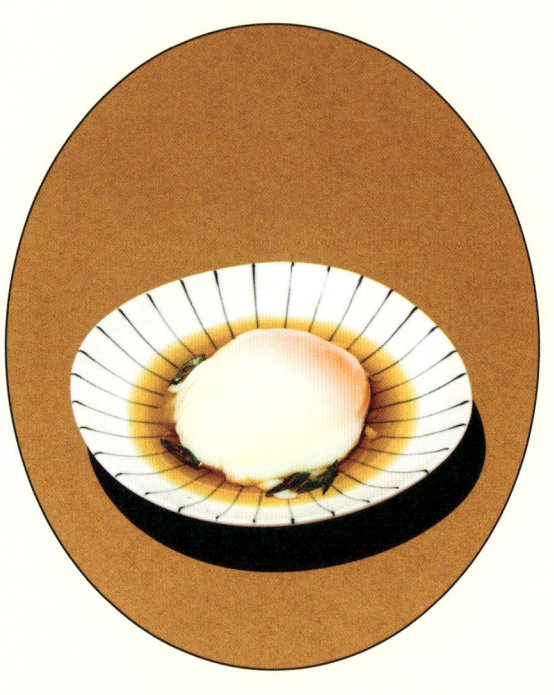

Makes 4 portions

4 eggs, at room temperature	
125 ml (½ cup) soy sauce	
60 ml (¼ cup) mirin	
60 ml (¼ cup) sake	
3 teaspoons caster (superfine) sugar	
1 garlic clove, smashed	

Place the eggs in a saucepan of boiling water and boil for 6 minutes. Drain and plunge into an ice bath.

Meanwhile, combine the remaining ingredients in a saucepan over medium heat and simmer for 1–2 minutes, until the sugar has dissolved. Remove from the heat, transfer to a heatproof bowl and set aside to cool completely.

Peel the eggs and place them in the cooled soy sauce mixture, turning to coat them all over. Cover and refrigerate for 4–5 hours, or up to 12 hours. The longer you leave the eggs, the stronger the flavour will be.

Cut the eggs in half and serve with your ramen of choice. You can either discard the soy sauce mixture or use it to season your ramen.

Makes 4 portions

4 eggs, at room temperature	
2 tablespoons mirin	
1 teaspoon caster (superfine) sugar	
125 ml (½ cup) light soy sauce	
250 ml (1 cup) cold Dashi Stock	P.33
1 spring onion (scallion), finely sliced	

Using a digital thermometer to assist you, heat a large saucepan of water to exactly 75°C (165°F). Place the eggs in the pan and cook at this temperature for 13 minutes. Transfer to an ice bath to stop the cooking process.

Meanwhile, combine the mirin, sugar and soy sauce in a saucepan over medium heat and simmer for 1–2 minutes, until the sugar has dissolved.

Pour the mirin mixture into the dashi stock and stir to combine. Divide the liquid among four small bowls, add a peeled egg to each bowl and garnish with a little spring onion. Serve alongside your ramen of choice.

うま味椎茸粉
Umami Shiitake Ko
UMAMI MUSHROOM POWDER

Makes 85 g (⅔ cup)

20 g (¾ oz) dried shiitake mushrooms

40 g (⅓ cup) sea salt flakes

1 tablespoon Korean chilli powder (gochugaru)

½ teaspoon black peppercorns

Place all the ingredients in a spice grinder and pulverise to a powder.

Sprinkle over ramen, eggs, veggies ... just about anything and everything for a spiced umami hit.

The mixture will keep in a glass jar in the pantry for up to 6 months.

黒マー油
Kuro Ma-yu
BLACK GARLIC OIL

Makes about 160 ml (⅔ cup)

80 ml (⅓ cup) peanut oil

1 garlic bulb, cloves peeled and chopped

80 ml (⅓ cup) toasted sesame oil

1 tablespoon toasted black sesame seeds

pinch of sea salt

Warm the peanut oil in a frying pan over medium heat and slowly cook the garlic until the garlic starts to brown. Reduce the heat to low and continue cooking for 7–8 minutes, until the garlic blackens. Remove from the heat.

Transfer the garlic and oil mixture to a blender. Add the sesame oil, sesame seeds and salt and process until smooth. Allow to cool before straining through a fine sieve into a sterilised jar.

Drizzle black garlic oil over your ramen of choice.

It will keep in an airtight container in the fridge for 1½–2 months.

45

TOPPINGS & EXTRAS

When in doubt, just add chashu. A Japanese adaption of Chinese char siu (barbecued pork), chashu is melt-in-your-mouth pork belly, slowly braised until fork tender. While Chinese char siu is roasted in a sweet marinade of hoisin, honey and soy sauce, Japanese chashu is gently simmered in a flavourful broth of soy sauce, mirin and sugar.

ポーク焼豚

Poku Chashu

CHASHU PORK

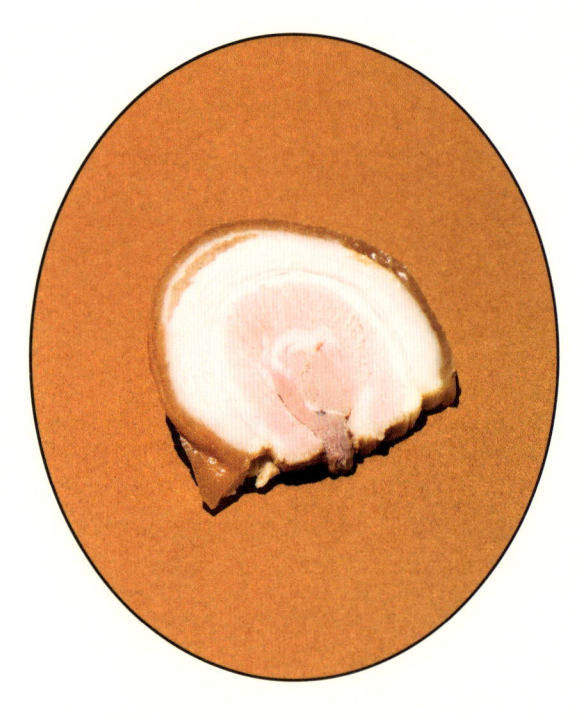

Makes 8 portions

1 kg (2 lb 3 oz) boneless pork belly, skin on
250 ml (1 cup) sake
250 ml (1 cup) mirin
125 ml (½ cup) soy sauce
110 g (½ cup) caster (superfine) sugar
4 spring onions (scallions), quartered
2 Asian shallots, halved
6 garlic cloves, smashed
20 g (¾ oz) ginger, sliced

Preheat the oven to 135°C (275°F).

Roll up the pork belly with the skin on the outside. Tie with kitchen string, at 2 cm (¾ in) intervals along the pork.

Place the remaining ingredients and 500 ml (2 cups) water in a flameproof casserole dish (Dutch oven) and bring to the boil. Remove from the heat and add the pork.

Cover and transfer to the oven for 4–5 hours, turning the pork occasionally, until completely cooked through and tender.

Cool the pork and the braising liquid to room temperature. Cover and leave to rest in the fridge overnight to achieve maximum flavour.

Remove the pork from the braising liquid, finely slice and serve on your ramen of choice.

The braising liquid can be used as the Ajitsuke Tamago marinade (page 44) or as a tare seasoning for your ramen.

The sliced chashu and liquid will keep in airtight containers in the fridge for 5–6 days.

Patience is key when it comes to perfecting this shredded pork shoulder recipe. When we say it's fork tender, we mean it – the pork should be so soft it can be effortlessly shredded with a fork. This pork recipe is a leaner alternative to chashu, pairing particularly well with lighter broths such as shio and shoyu ramen.

豚肩肉のみじん切り
Butakataniku No Mijingiri
SHREDDED PORK SHOULDER

Makes 8 portions

1.5 kg (3 lb 5 oz) pork shoulder, bone in, skin removed

500 ml (2 cups) chicken stock

250 ml (1 cup) soy sauce

2 tablespoons toasted sesame oil

4 garlic cloves, crushed

20 g (¾ oz) ginger, sliced

Dry Rub

2½ teaspoons shichimi togarashi (see note)

2 teaspoons sea salt

2 teaspoons freshly ground black pepper

2 teaspoons brown sugar

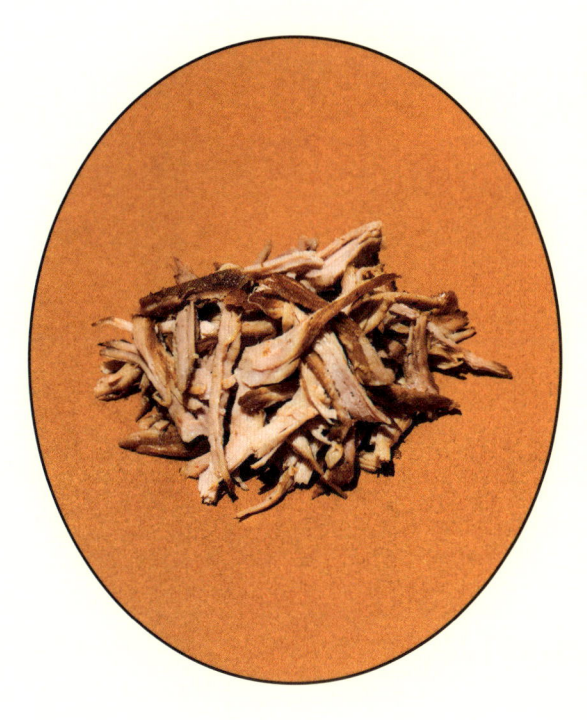

Combine the dry rub ingredients in a bowl and massage over the pork shoulder.

Transfer the pork to a slow cooker and add the remaining ingredients. Cover and cook on low for about 8 hours, until the pork comes away easily from the bone when tested with a fork. Remove the meat from the slow cooker and shred with two forks.

Serve the pork on your ramen of choice and use the braising liquid as a spicy tare.

The shredded pork and braising liquid will keep in airtight containers in the fridge for 5–6 days, or in the freezer for up to 3 months.

You can also remove the fat that solidifies on top of the braising liquid to use in your ramen for that extra fat flavour bomb.

(NOTE) Shichimi togarashi can be purchased from most Asian supermarkets.

TOPPINGS & EXTRAS

Kakuni, meaning 'square simmered', refers to both the shape and the braising method of this popular ramen topping. Originating from Chinese dongpo pork, these melt-in-your-mouth pork belly cubes were introduced to the port city of Nagasaki by Chinese merchants and adapted to suit local tastes. Kakuni is typically served with karashi (Japanese mustard) and pickled vegetables to balance the sweetness.

角煮
Kakuni
BRAISED PORK BELLY

Makes 4 portions

1 kg (2 lb 3 oz) pork belly, cut into 5 cm (2 in) cubes

30 g (1 oz) ginger, sliced

½ onion, quartered

2 spring onions (scallions), quartered

½ teaspoon sea salt

Braising Liquid

500 ml (2 cups) Dashi Stock P.33

125 ml (½ cup) sake

80 ml (⅓ cup) soy sauce

60 ml (¼ cup) mirin

15 g (½ oz) ginger, sliced

2 tablespoons brown sugar

Sear the pork belly cubes in a large frying pan over medium–high heat until golden brown on all sides.

Transfer to a saucepan and add the ginger, onion, spring onion, salt and 2 litres (8 cups) water and bring to the boil. Reduce the heat to a simmer and cook for 2½–3 hours, until the pork is cooked through and tender. Remove the pork from the pan and discard the braising liquid.

Place all the braising ingredients in a clean saucepan over medium–low heat and add the pork. Simmer for 50–60 minutes, until the pork is meltingly tender; there should be about 250 ml (1 cup) of liquid remaining. Remove the pork from the liquid and serve on your ramen of choice.

The remaining braising liquid can be used as a tare to flavour your ramen broth, if you like.

The pork will keep in an airtight container in the fridge for 5–6 days.

トッピングとつけ合わせ

An essential component of any traditional meal, Japanese pickles – tsukemono – are found in everything from breakfast bento boxes to evening ramen bowls. The art of pickling is surprisingly simple, with the same brine working wonders on any type of vegetable, such as cucumber, cabbage or daikon. These quick pickles cleanse the palate and add a satisfying crunch to dishes, making it easy to finish an entire bowl of ramen in one go.

漬物
Tsukemono
JAPANESE QUICK PICKLES

Makes about 680 ml (23 fl oz)

175 g (1½ cups) finely sliced radishes

1 umeboshi plum

1 small red chilli, halved

½ garlic clove, sliced (optional)

250 ml (1 cup) rice wine vinegar

2 tablespoons caster (superfine) sugar

2 teaspoons fine sea salt

5 black peppercorns

Place the radish slices in a heatproof bowl with the plum, chilli and garlic, if using.

Pour the vinegar and 250 ml (1 cup) water into a saucepan. Add the sugar, salt and peppercorns and place over medium heat, stirring to dissolve the sugar and salt. Bring to the boil, then pour over the vegetables and leave to cool.

Serve alongside ramen, pork dishes and cold noodle salads.

The pickles will keep in an airtight container in the fridge for up to 1 week.

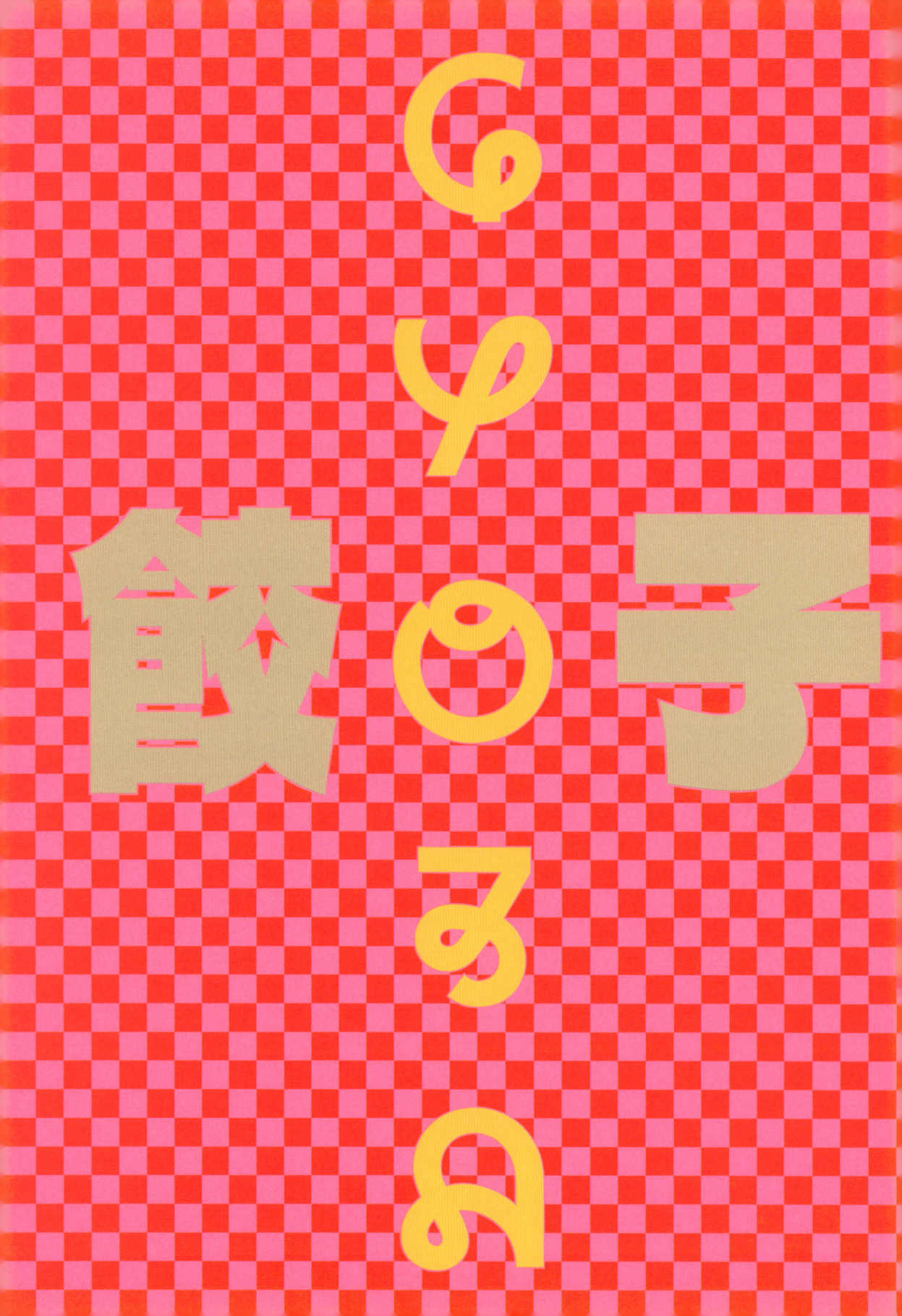

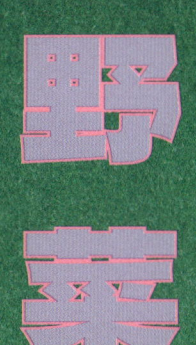

野菜

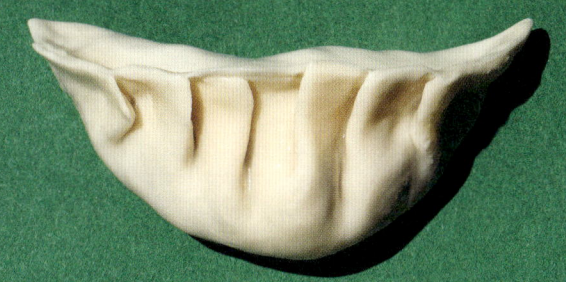

Vegetable Gyoza

シーフード

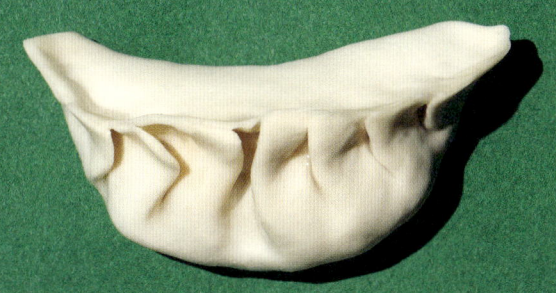

Seafood Gyoza

ポーク

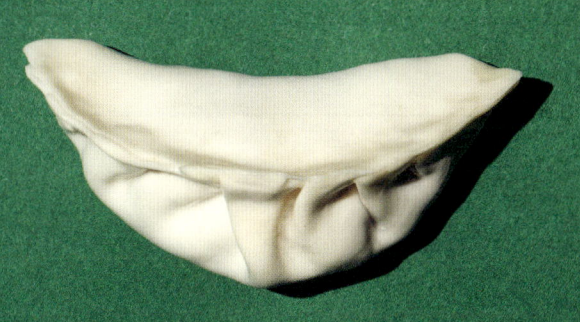

Pork Gyoza

Whether pan-fried, boiled or steamed, these versatile dumplings are a staple of Japan's vibrant street food scene. Inspired by Chinese jiaozi dumplings, gyozas were introduced to Japan in the post–World War II period during the 1940s and 50s. While regional variations of fillings and dipping sauces exist, their status as a favourite ramen topping holds strong throughout Japan.

野菜餃子
Yasai Gyoza
VEGETABLE GYOZAS

Makes 25

2 teaspoons toasted sesame oil

peanut oil, for pan-frying

100 g (3½ oz) mixed fresh mushrooms, such as shiitake, wood ear and king brown, finely chopped

100 g (3½ oz) cabbage, finely shredded

100 g (3½ oz) firm tofu, crumbled

2 spring onions (scallions), finely sliced

2 garlic cloves, finely grated

1 tablespoon finely grated ginger

1 bird's eye chilli, seeded and finely sliced

1 egg white

2 teaspoons soy sauce

2 teaspoons sake

1 teaspoon toasted sesame oil

½ teaspoon sea salt

¼ teaspoon ground white pepper

25 gyoza wrappers

Heat the sesame oil and 1 teaspoon peanut oil in a wok over medium heat.

Add the mushrooms and cabbage and sauté for 1–2 minutes. Transfer to a heatproof bowl and set aside to cool. Add the remaining ingredients, except the gyoza wrappers, and mix to combine.

Place a scant tablespoon of filling onto the middle of a gyoza wrapper and lightly brush half the edges with water. Fold the wrapper over the filling and crimp the edges together, making 4–5 pleats to seal. Repeat with the remaining filling and wrappers.

Warm 2 tablespoons peanut oil in a frying pan over medium–high heat. Working in batches, add the gyozas, frying on one side for 2–3 minutes, until the bottoms turn golden brown. Add 3 tablespoons water to the pan, cover immediately and steam for about 3 minutes, or until the water has evaporated. Repeat with the remaining gyozas, adding more peanut oil as necessary.

Serve hot, either in your ramen of choice, or on the side.

Any remaining uncooked gyozas will keep in an airtight container, layered between baking paper, in the freezer for up to 3 months.

トッピングとつけ合わせ

Shifudo Gyoza

SEAFOOD GYOZAS

Makes 25

300 g (10½ oz) raw prawn (shrimp) meat, roughly chopped

20 g (¾ oz) garlic chives, roughly chopped

1 tablespoon sake

1 tablespoon soy sauce

1 teaspoon toasted sesame oil

1½ tablespoons grated ginger

2 garlic cloves, grated

⅓ teaspoon sea salt

pinch of ground white pepper

1 egg white

25 gyoza wrappers

peanut oil, for pan-frying

Place all the ingredients, except the gyoza wrappers and peanut oil, in a food processor. Pulse until combined.

Place a scant tablespoon of filling onto the middle of a gyoza wrapper and lightly brush half the edges with water. Fold the wrapper over the filling and crimp the edges together, making 4–5 pleats to seal. Repeat with the remaining filling and wrappers.

Warm 2 tablespoons peanut oil in a frying pan over medium–high heat. Working in batches, add the gyozas, frying on one side for 2–3 minutes, until the bottoms turn golden brown. Add 3 tablespoons water to the pan, cover immediately and steam for about 3 minutes, or until the water has evaporated. Repeat with the remaining gyozas, adding more peanut oil as necessary.

Serve hot, either in your ramen of choice, or on the side.

Any remaining uncooked gyozas will keep in an airtight container, layered between baking paper, in the freezer for up to 3 months.

Poku Gyoza

PORK GYOZAS

Makes 25

200 g (7 oz) minced (ground) pork

100 g (3½ oz) cabbage, finely shredded

2 spring onions (scallions), finely sliced

1½ tablespoons finely grated ginger

2 garlic cloves, finely grated

½ teaspoon freshly ground black pepper

½ teaspoon sea salt

1 teaspoon toasted sesame oil

1 egg white

25 gyoza wrappers

peanut oil, for pan-frying

Place all the ingredients, except the gyoza wrappers and peanut oil, in a food processor. Pulse until combined.

Place a scant tablespoon of filling onto the middle of a gyoza wrapper and lightly brush half the edges with water. Fold the wrapper over the filling and crimp the edges together, making 4–5 pleats to seal. Repeat with the remaining filling and wrappers.

Warm 2 tablespoons peanut oil in a frying pan over medium–high heat. Working in batches, add the gyozas, frying on one side for 2–3 minutes, until the bottoms turn golden brown. Add 3 tablespoons water to the pan, cover immediately and steam for about 3 minutes, or until the water has evaporated. Repeat with the remaining gyozas, adding more peanut oil as necessary.

Serve hot, either in your ramen of choice, or on the side.

Any remaining uncooked gyozas will keep in an airtight container, layered between baking paper, in the freezer for up to 3 months.

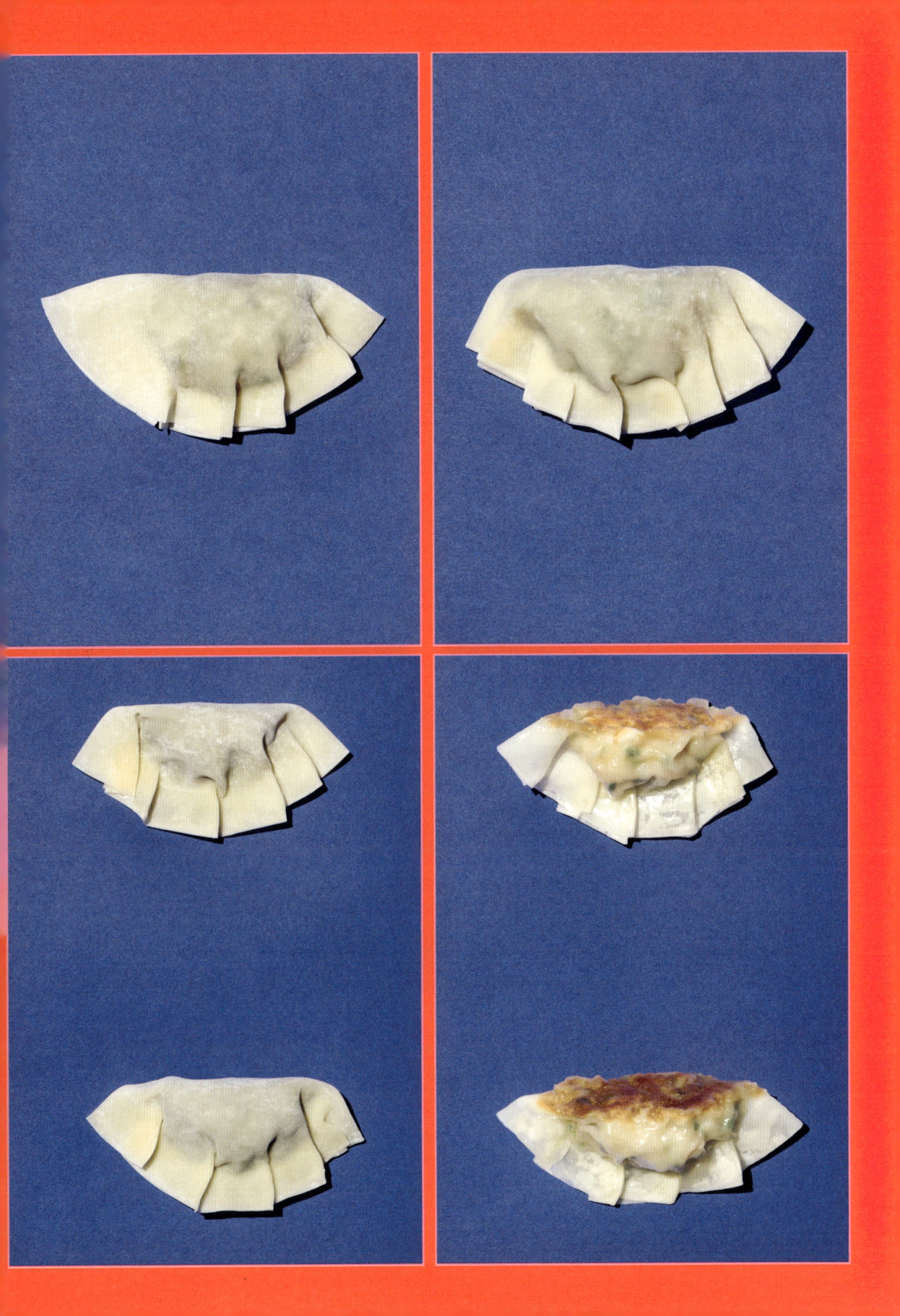

With its signature pink swirl, this iconic fish cake is so popular that it even has its own emoji. The name *narutomaki* references Naruto, the city where it originated, with the swirl pattern reminiscent of whirlpools found in the Naruto Strait. Narutomaki adds a playful pop of colour to a typically achromatic bowl of meat and broth.

なると巻

Narutomaki

FISH CAKES

Makes 16 × 1 cm (½ in) slices

250 g (9 oz) skinless white fish fillet, pin-boned and roughly chopped

1 teaspoon fine sea salt

1 teaspoon caster (superfine) sugar

1 teaspoon mirin

1 egg white

pinch of ground white pepper

3–4 drops red food colouring

Place the fish in a bowl of cold water and leave to soak for 3–4 minutes. Rinse and drain well, squeezing out any excess water.

Transfer to a food processor, along with the salt, sugar, mirin, egg white and pepper. Process to a fine paste.

Cover a bamboo sushi mat with plastic wrap. Using a spatula, spread out three-quarters of the fish mixture on top of the plastic wrap to form an 18 cm × 12 cm (7 in × 4¾ in) rectangle. Mix the food colouring into the remaining fish mixture and spread this on top.

Carefully roll the sushi mat away from you to shape the fish mixture into a log. Tightly twist the ends of the plastic wrap to encase the mixture.

Bring a large saucepan of water to the boil and place a bamboo steamer over the top. Place the narutomaki in the steamer and steam for about 20 minutes, until cooked through.

Leave to cool to room temperature before slicing into 1 cm (½ in) pieces and adding to your ramen of choice.

Narutomaki will keep in an airtight container in the fridge for up to 5 days, or in the freezer for up to 3 months.

トッピングとつけ合わせ TOPPINGS & EXTRAS

With 2000 years under its belt, kimchi is a timeless Korean staple that's only gotten better with age. Originally called *chimchae*, translating to 'soaked vegetables', it was traditionally made with napa cabbage and radishes soaked in brine or beef stock. However, the kimchi we know today is fermented with chilli, imparting its signature spicy tang.

キムチ
Kimchi

Makes 1 litre (4 cups)

1 kg (2 lb 3 oz) wombok (Chinese cabbage), sliced into 4 cm (1½ in) strips

80 g (2¾ oz) sea salt

1.5 litres (6 cups) filtered water

5 garlic cloves, finely grated

30 g (1 oz) ginger, finely grated

200 g (7 oz) daikon, julienned

4 spring onions (scallions), finely sliced

1 tablespoon dried shrimp (see note)

3 tablespoons Korean chilli powder (gochugaru)

2 tablespoons soy sauce

2 tablespoons fish sauce

Place the cabbage in a large glass bowl and sprinkle with the salt. Using your hands, rub the salt into the cabbage. Cover with the filtered water and leave to macerate for 2–3 hours. Drain and rinse the cabbage, squeezing out any remaining water.

Place the cabbage back in the glass bowl and mix in the garlic, ginger, daikon, spring onion and dried shrimp.

In a small bowl, mix together the chilli powder, soy sauce and fish sauce. Pour this over the cabbage mixture and thoroughly combine, using gloves if mixing by hand. Taste and add more chilli powder if desired.

Tightly pack the kimchi into a 1 litre (4 cup) sterilised jar – the vegetables should be completely submerged in the liquid. Add water if necessary, then seal and leave at room temperature, out of direct sunlight, to ferment for 1–5 days. The longer you leave the kimchi, the stronger the flavour will be. Transfer to the fridge, where the kimchi will keep for 4–5 months.

Serve the kimchi in your ramen of choice, or alongside.

(NOTE) To make vegan kimchi, omit the dried shrimp and fish sauce and replace with 2 tablespoons dulse flakes or one finely ground nori sheet.

トッピングとつけ合わせ TOPPINGS & EXTRAS

ガーリックチップス
Ga-rikku Chipusu
GARLIC CHIPS

わかめごま塩
Wakame Gomasio
WAKAME SESAME SALT

**Makes about 50 g (½ cup) garlic chips
and about 140 ml (4½ fl oz) garlic oil**

1 garlic bulb (about 50 g/1¾ oz), peeled

170 ml (⅔ cup) peanut oil

2 teaspoons toasted sesame oil

Finely slice the garlic cloves lengthways,
evenly and uniformly, so they are all the same
thickness – this will ensure even cooking.

Warm the oils in a frying pan over low heat
and slowly fry the garlic for 6–7 minutes,
until golden and crisp. Remove from the oil
and drain on paper towel, reserving the oil.

The garlic chips will keep in an airtight
container for 1–2 days, but they are best used
the same day.

The garlic oil will keep in a sealed jar
in the fridge for about 2 months.

Makes about 180 g (1½ cups)

1 piece of dried wakame (about 6–7 g/¼ oz)

155 g (1 cup) sesame seeds

2 tablespoons sea salt flakes

Preheat the oven to 160°C (320°F). Place the
wakame on a baking tray and toast in the oven
for 9–10 minutes. Set aside to cool completely.

Meanwhile, toast the sesame seeds in a
heavy-based frying pan over very low heat for
5–6 minutes, until they take on a deep golden
brown colour and a buttery aroma. Remove
from the pan and set aside to cool completely.

Place the sesame seeds, wakame and
salt in a food processor and pulse for about
30 seconds, until the ingredients are
quite finely ground but there are still a few
whole seeds.

Sprinkle wakame gomasio over your
favourite ramen toppings, or blend into
your broth of choice.

It will keep in a sealed jar in the pantry
for up to 3 weeks.

トッピングとつけ合わせ

ふりかけ
Furikake

Makes about 80 g (2¾ oz)

40 g (¼ cup) sesame seeds

2 tablespoons black sesame seeds

3 nori sheets

4 g (¼ cup) bonito flakes (katsuobushi)

2 teaspoons sea salt flakes

1 teaspoon caster (superfine) sugar (optional)

Toast the sesame seeds in a heavy-based frying pan over very low heat for 5–6 minutes, until they take on a deep golden brown colour and a buttery aroma. Remove from the pan and set aside to cool completely.

Place all the ingredients in a food processor and pulse to blend.

Sprinkle furikake over your ramen of choice; it is also delicious on rice.

It will keep in a sealed jar in the pantry for 1–2 months.

椎茸のうま煮
Shiitake No Umani
PICKLED SHIITAKE MUSHROOMS

Makes about 230 g (8 oz)

125 ml (½ cup) soy sauce or tamari

125 ml (½ cup) rice wine vinegar

55 g (¼ cup) caster (superfine) sugar

3 thin slices peeled ginger

1 small red chilli, sliced in half

230 g (8 oz) rehydrated shiitake mushrooms

Pour the soy sauce, vinegar and 125 ml (½ cup) water into a small saucepan. Add the sugar, ginger and chilli and whisk over low–medium heat until the sugar has dissolved.

Place the mushrooms in a heatproof bowl and pour the pickling liquid over them. Set aside to cool, then cover and refrigerate.

The mushrooms will be ready to use in about 3 hours and will keep in an airtight container in the fridge for 1 week.

Serve alongside pork dishes, ramen and cold noodle salads.

61

ラード
Ra-do
RENDERED PORK FAT

Makes about 260 g (1¼ cups)

500 g (1 lb 2 oz) organic pork fat, cut into
3 cm (1¼ in) cubes

Place the pork fat in a heavy-based
saucepan, pour in 125 ml (½ cup) water
and cook over low heat for 4–5 hours. Stir
occasionally and ensure the heat is gentle
enough to melt the fat instead of charring it.
During this time the water will evaporate and
the fat will slowly render into liquid, leaving
behind small, golden brown chunks of fat.

Drain the liquid through a fine-meshed
sieve into a sterilised jar, discarding the
solids. The liquid will be a light yellow colour
but will change to pure white when solidified.

The rendered pork fat will keep in an
airtight container in the fridge for up
to 3 months, or in the freezer for up to
6 months.

Use in ramen broths and tares, and as
a frying oil.

NOTE You can also render the pork fat in
a slow cooker. Put the lid on and cook on
low for 7–8 hours.

佃煮
Tsukudani
SWEET BRAISED KOMBU

Makes about 45 g (1½ oz)

2 large pieces of kombu, each about 6.5 cm × 17.5 cm (2½ in × 7 in), julienned (see note)	
2 tablespoons soy sauce	
1 tablespoon mirin	
3 teaspoons rice wine vinegar	
1½ tablespoons caster (superfine) sugar	
250 ml (1 cup) Dashi Stock	P.33
1 teaspoon toasted sesame seeds	

Place the kombu in a saucepan with the soy
sauce, mirin, vinegar, sugar and dashi stock.
Bring to the boil, then reduce the heat and
simmer for 25–35 minutes, until the mixture
has reduced to a thick sticky glaze just
coating the kombu.

Sprinkle in the sesame seeds and stir
them through.

Serve alongside ramen, rice or pork dishes.

The tsukudani will keep in a sealed jar
in the fridge for up to 1 week.

NOTE Instead of dried kombu, you can use
rehydrated kombu from making the Dashi
Stock on page 33.

味噌バター爆弾
Miso Bata-Bakudan
MISO BUTTER BOMBS

のりバター爆弾
Nori Bata-Bakudan
SEAWEED BUTTER BOMBS

Makes about 390 g (14 oz)

250 g (9 oz) butter, softened

135 g (5 oz) white miso paste

2 garlic cloves, finely grated

1 teaspoon ponzu

Place all the ingredients in a food processor and blitz to combine.

Chill in the fridge, then roll into small balls (bombs) to add to your ramen.

The mixture can also be rolled into a log shape, encased in baking paper or plastic wrap and stored in the freezer for up to 3 months. Slice off portions as required, then melt over corn in ramen or vegetables and fish.

Makes about 280 g (10 oz)

2 nori sheets

250 g (9 oz) butter, softened, or Rendered Pork Fat   P.62

1 teaspoon lemon zest

2 garlic cloves, finely grated

1 teaspoon toasted sesame seeds

½ teaspoon shichimi togarashi (see note)

¼ teaspoon toasted sesame oil

¼ teaspoon soy sauce

Crumble the nori sheets into a food processor and pulse until finely chopped. Add the remaining ingredients and blitz to combine.

Chill in the fridge, then roll into small balls (bombs) to add to your ramen.

The mixture can also be rolled into a log shape, encased in baking paper or plastic wrap and stored in the freezer for up to 3 months. Slice off portions as required, then melt over corn in ramen or vegetables and fish.

NOTE Shichimi togarashi can be purchased from most Asian supermarkets.

味噌
ラーメン

This East-meets-West ramen remix gives your morning bacon and eggs a tasty Japanese twist. Drawing inspiration from Hokkaido, the sweet, buttery corn in this ramen balances the rich, savoury broth, while smoky bacon and jammy eggs add a comforting touch of Western flair. It's an easy way to win the morning.

Miso Ramen

Buttered Corn, Bacon and Ajitsuke Tamago Ramen

Serves 2

4 slices smoked bacon	
2 portions Ramen Noodles, cooked al dente and drained	P.37
800 ml (27 fl oz) Miso Broth, simmering	P.23
2 Ajitsuke Tamago, halved	P.44
10 slices menma	
100 g (3½ oz) fresh corn kernels, blanched	
2 Miso Butter Bombs	P.63
2 spring onions (scallions), finely sliced	
2 teaspoons toasted black sesame seeds	

Put the bacon in a cold cast-iron frying pan and place over medium–high heat (this renders the bacon evenly). Fry for about 8 minutes, until well cooked and crisp, then chop into bite-sized pieces.

To assemble the ramen, quickly and evenly divide the warm drained noodles between two bowls and pour the hot miso broth over. Add the bacon, ajitsuke tamago, menma and corn. Dot the corn with a miso butter bomb and garnish with the spring onion and sesame seeds. Drizzle some of the bacon fat from the pan over the ramen for extra flavour and serve straight away.

味噌
ラーメン

Can't decide which ramen to make? This miso masterpiece will seal the deal for all the indecisive ramen fans, bringing together seafood, meat and veggies in one hearty bowl. The spicy kick from the prawn sauce cuts through the rich, chashu-infused broth, while earthy mushrooms add an extra layer of umami flavour. We won't judge if you go back for seconds.

Miso Ramen

Spicy Prawn, Chashu Pork and Enoki Mushroom Ramen

Serves 2

8 raw prawns (shrimp), shelled with tails left intact, deveined	
1 tablespoon peanut oil	
6 slices Chashu Pork	P.46
800 ml (27 fl oz) Miso Broth, simmering	P.23
2 portions Ramen Noodles, cooked al dente and drained	P.37
30 g (1 oz) enoki mushrooms	
10 slices menma	
2 teaspoons toasted sesame seeds	
3 teaspoons shio kombu (see notes)	

Prawn Sauce
2 teaspoons finely grated ginger
1 garlic clove, finely grated
1 spring onion (scallion), finely sliced
1–2 tablespoons spicy chilli bean paste (la doubanjiang), to taste (see notes)
2 teaspoons rice wine vinegar
1 teaspoon toasted sesame oil

Combine the prawn sauce ingredients in a bowl and mix well. Add the prawns and toss well to coat.

Heat the oil in a frying pan over medium heat and fry the prawns for 2–3 minutes, until just cooked. Remove from the heat and keep warm.

Place the chashu slices into the simmering miso broth to gently warm, or warm through in the chashu braising liquid.

To assemble the ramen, quickly and evenly divide the warm drained noodles between two bowls and pour the hot miso broth over. Add the chashu pork slices, spicy prawns, enoki mushrooms and menma. Sprinkle with the sesame seeds and shio kombu to garnish and serve straight away.

(NOTES) Shio kombu is a seaweed garnish available from most Japanese grocery stores.

La doubanjiang can be purchased from most Asian supermarkets.

味噌

ラーメン

We like to think of this ocean-kissed ramen as Japan's answer to Italy's frutti di mare (seafood pasta). In the 1970s and 80s, Japanese chefs began experimenting with seafood-based broths to intensify the natural umami flavour of their soups, incorporating dashi made from kombu or dried bonito flakes. Topped with juicy prawns, mussels and scallops, this bowl is a treasure trove of goodies.

Miso Ramen

Seafood
Ramen

Serves 2

3 teaspoons peanut oil	
1 garlic clove, smashed	
1 teaspoon finely grated ginger	
1 tablespoon Dashi Stock or water	P.33
12 mussels, scrubbed and debearded	
6 raw prawns (shrimp), shelled and deveined	
6 scallops	
800 ml (27 fl oz) Miso Broth, simmering	P.23
2 portions Ramen Noodles, cooked al dente and drained	P.37
20 g (¾ oz) fresh wood ear mushrooms, sliced	
4 slices Narutomaki	P.57
1 nori sheet, cut into quarters	
2 Seaweed Butter Bombs	P.63
2 tablespoons finely shaved bonito flakes (hanakatsuo)	

Heat 2 teaspoons of the oil in a wok over medium–high heat. Stir-fry the garlic and ginger for 1–2 minutes. Add the dashi stock or water and the mussels, then cover with a lid. Increase the heat to high and steam for 2–3 minutes, until the mussels have opened. Remove the pan from the heat and set aside.

Preheat a chargrill pan to medium–high.

Place the prawns and scallops in a bowl and toss the remaining oil through to coat. Grill the prawns for 2–3 minutes and the scallops for 1–2 minutes, turning halfway, until just cooked through.

Add the cooked mussels and their residual liquid to the simmering miso broth.

To assemble the ramen, quickly and evenly divide the warm drained noodles between two bowls and pour the hot miso broth and mussels over. Add the prawns, scallops, mushrooms, narutomaki, nori and butter bombs. Finish with a sprinkling of shaved bonito flakes.

味噌

ラーメン

Right up there with pho, laksa and pad thai, chashu pork ramen is easily one of the best bowls to come out of Asia. The umami-packed miso broth is amped up with meltingly tender braised chashu pork belly, fresh cabbage and crunchy bean sprouts. Can you handle the heat? We recommend a generous drizzle of fiery chilli oil to tie it all together.

Miso Ramen

Chashu Pork, Cabbage and Bean Sprout Ramen

Serves 2

1 teaspoon peanut oil	
1 teaspoon toasted sesame oil	
1 garlic clove, finely grated	
1 spring onion (scallion), finely sliced	
120 g (4½ oz) shredded cabbage	
50 g (1¾ oz) bean sprouts	
6 slices Chashu Pork	P.46
800 ml (27 fl oz) Miso Broth, simmering	P.23
2 portions Ramen Noodles, cooked al dente and drained	P.37
2 Ajitsuke Tamago, halved	P.44
20 g (¾ oz) pickled ginger (beni shoga)	
chilli oil, for drizzling	
Tsukudani, to serve	P.62

Heat the oils in a wok over high heat and stir-fry the garlic, spring onion, cabbage and bean sprouts for 1–2 minutes.

Place the chashu slices into the simmering broth to gently warm, or warm through in the chashu braising liquid.

To assemble the ramen, quickly and evenly divide the warm drained noodles between two bowls and pour the hot miso broth over. Add the chashu pork, stir-fried vegetables, ajitsuke tamago and pickled ginger. Finish with a drizzle of chilli oil and serve with tsukudani on the side.

73

味噌
ラーメン

Give your basic chicken noodle soup a serious upgrade with this simple, smoky miso ramen. This twist on classic chashu ramen gets its flavour from barbecued chicken, bringing the taste of Japan's yakitori (grilled chicken skewers) right into your bowl. The best part? You can use store-bought chicken or leftovers from last night's barbecue.

Miso Ramen

Barbecue Chicken Ramen

Serves 2

2 portions Ramen Noodles, cooked al dente and drained	P.37
100 g (3½ oz) finely shredded Chinese broccoli (gai lan)	
265 g (1½ cups) shredded store-bought barbecued chicken	
800 ml (27 fl oz) Miso Broth, simmering	P.23
2 Ajitsuke Tamago, halved	P.44
100 g (3½ oz) fresh corn kernels, blanched	
2 teaspoons cold butter	
2 teaspoons shichimi togarashi (see note)	
Furikake, to garnish	P.61

To assemble the ramen, quickly and evenly divide the warm drained noodles between two bowls and add the broccoli and barbecued chicken. Pour the hot miso broth over and add the ajitsuke tamago and corn. Dot the corn with the butter and sprinkle with the shichimi togarashi. Garnish with furikake and serve straight away.

(NOTE) Shichimi togarashi can be purchased from most Asian supermarkets.

Rich, fatty and totally irresistible, kakuni is a specialty hailing from Japan's southern island of Kyushu. The word *kakuni* translates to 'square simmered', which perfectly describes these succulent cubes of slow-cooked skinless pork belly, braised in a sweet–salty sauce until they're fall-apart tender. This is comfort food at its finest.

Miso Ramen

Kakuni Ramen

Serves 2

3 teaspoons peanut oil	
1 garlic clove, finely grated	
50 g (1¾ oz) snow pea (mangetout) tendrils	
50 g (1¾ oz) bean sprouts	
pinch of caster (superfine) sugar	
pinch of sea salt	
1 teaspoon Chinese rice wine	
1 teaspoon toasted sesame oil	
2 portions Ramen Noodles, cooked al dente and drained	P.37
800 ml (27 fl oz) Miso Broth, simmering	P.23
8–10 pieces of Kakuni, warmed	P.48
2 teaspoons spicy chilli bean paste (la doubanjiang), or to taste (see note)	
20 g (¾ oz) pickled ginger (beni shoga)	
Garlic Chips, to garnish	P.60

Heat the peanut oil in a wok over medium–low heat and slowly fry the garlic, taking care not to burn it. Add the snow pea tendrils and bean sprouts, increase the heat to medium and toss to combine. Add the sugar, salt, rice wine and sesame oil and toss for 1–2 minutes. Remove from the heat.

To assemble the ramen, quickly and evenly divide the warm drained noodles between two bowls and pour the hot miso broth over. Add the stir-fried vegetables, kakuni, chilli bean paste and pickled ginger. Sprinkle with the garlic chips and serve straight away.

NOTE La doubanjiang can be purchased from most Asian supermarkets.

77

Fun fact: did you know miso is naturally plant-based? The fermented soy bean paste lays the groundwork for this incredibly wholesome vegetarian ramen. Smoky tofu mimics the savoury depth typically provided by meat, while the naturally sweet miso-glazed vegetables take a cue from Japan's classic nasu dengaku (miso-glazed eggplant).

Miso Ramen

Smoked Tofu, Miso-glazed Carrots and Eggplant Ramen

Serves 2

2 tablespoons white miso paste	
2 tablespoons mirin	
1 tablespoon sake	
1 teaspoon caster (superfine) sugar	
1½ tablespoons peanut oil	
2 teaspoons toasted sesame oil	
150 g (5½ oz) Japanese eggplant (aubergine), cut into 3 cm (1¼ in) cubes	
120 g (4½ oz) carrot, julienned	
2 portions Ramen Noodles, cooked al dente and drained	P.37
800 ml (27 fl oz) Vegan Broth, simmering	P.31
200 g (7 oz) smoked tofu, cut into 6 slices	
50 g (1¾ oz) bean sprouts	
2 teaspoons toasted sesame seeds	
chilli oil, for drizzling	
Umami Mushroom Powder, to garnish	P.45

In a small bowl, whisk together the miso paste, mirin, sake and sugar.

Heat the oils in a wok over medium–high heat and stir-fry the eggplant for about 2 minutes. Add the carrot and stir-fry for a further minute. Add the miso mixture and stir-fry for another minute.

To assemble the ramen, quickly and evenly divide the warm drained noodles between two bowls and pour the hot vegan broth over. Add the vegetables, smoked tofu, bean sprouts and sesame seeds. Drizzle with the chilli oil, garnish with the mushroom powder and serve straight away.

Karaage and ramen – can you name a better duo? These two dishes are at the heart of Japan's global food craze. Combine them and you get this modern spin on traditional shoyu ramen – a soy-based noodle soup that made its way from China to Japan in the late 19th century. Crispy on the outside and soft on the inside, the pork karaage makes this ramen dish distinctly Japanese.

Shoyu Ramen

Pork Karaage Ramen

Serves 2

2 teaspoons dried wakame	
2 portions Ramen Noodles, cooked al dente and drained	P.37
800 ml (27 fl oz) Shoyu Broth, simmering	P.25
2 slices Narutomaki	P.57
20 g (¾ oz) enoki mushrooms	
1 Ajitsuke Tamago, halved	P.44
2 spring onions (scallions), finely sliced	
Japanese Quick Pickles, to serve	P.49

Pork Karaage

2 garlic cloves, finely grated
10 g (¼ oz) ginger, finely grated
1 tablespoon soy sauce
1½ tablespoons sake
2 teaspoons toasted sesame oil
300 g (10½ oz) pork loin, cut into 4 cm (1½ in) pieces
peanut oil, for deep-frying
80 g (½ cup) potato starch
¼ teaspoon sea salt
¼ teaspoon ground white pepper

Rinse the wakame and rehydrate in a bowl of cold water. Drain well.

To make the pork karaage, combine the garlic, ginger, soy sauce, sake and sesame oil in a bowl. Add the pork and stir to coat, then cover and refrigerate for 30 minutes.

Heat enough oil for deep-frying in a deep-fryer, large saucepan or wok to 190°C (375°F).

Combine the potato starch, salt and pepper in a bowl. Remove the pork from the fridge, draining off and discarding the marinade. Toss the pork through the seasoned potato starch, coating thoroughly.

Fry the pork in batches for 3–4 minutes, until cooked through. Drain on a wire rack.

To assemble the ramen, quickly and evenly divide the warm drained noodles between two bowls and pour the hot shoyu broth over. Add the wakame, narutomaki, enoki mushrooms, ajitsuke tamago and spring onion. Top with the pork karaage and serve with Japanese pickles on the side.

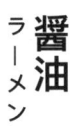

醤油
ラーメン

Renowned for its exceptional marbling and melt-in-your-mouth tenderness, Japanese wagyu takes this humble street food to a new level of luxury. Once reserved only for high-end restaurants, the tender beef brings a soft, velvety texture to every spoonful. Go all out on the gourmet toppings, including micro herbs, fresh wasabi and garlic chips.

Shoyu Ramen

Wagyu
Ramen

Serves 2

50–60 g (1¾–2 oz) fresh wagyu sirloin	
peanut oil, for deep-frying	
60 g (2 oz) leek, white part only, sliced	
2 portions Ramen Noodles, cooked al dente and drained	P.37
800 ml (27 fl oz) Shoyu Broth, simmering	P.25
40 g (1½ oz) bean sprouts	
2 tablespoons roasted peanuts, chopped	
2 teaspoons finely sliced garlic chives	
2 tablespoons shiso micro herbs (see notes)	
freshly grated wasabi, to taste (see notes)	
Garlic Chips, to garnish	P.60

Tightly wrap the wagyu in plastic wrap and freeze for 1–2 hours, until semi-frozen.

Remove the plastic wrap and slice the wagyu across the grain into 2–3 mm (⅛ in) thick slices, carpaccio style. Set aside.

Heat enough oil for deep-frying in a deep-fryer, large saucepan or wok to 175°C (340°F). Add the leek and fry until golden brown and crisp. Drain on paper towel.

To assemble the ramen, quickly and evenly divide the warm drained noodles between two bowls and pour the hot shoyu broth over. Add the sliced wagyu, leek, bean sprouts, peanuts and garlic chives. Top with the shiso micro herbs and wasabi. Garnish with garlic chips and serve straight away.

85

(NOTES) Shio micro herbs and fresh wasabi can be found at most Asian supermarkets. Substitute small shiso leaves and fresh horseradish, if unavailable.

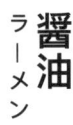
Vegos, this one's for you. The rise of plant-based diets in the 1990s and 2000s gave birth to revolutionary veg-friendly ramens that rival their meaty counterparts. In this bowl, Korean kimchi adds a tangy, spicy kick to the soy-based broth, perfectly balancing the mildness of the bean curd and zucchini.

Shoyu Ramen

Bean Curd, Zucchini and Kimchi Vegan Ramen

Serves 2

2 bean curd strands (see note)	
800 ml (27 fl oz) Vegan Broth, simmering	P.31
2 portions Ramen Noodles, cooked al dente and drained	P.37
100 g (3½ oz) zucchini (courgette), shredded or spiralised	
100 g (3½ oz) fresh corn kernels, blanched	
100 g (3½ oz) Kimchi	P.58
2 tablespoons kimchi juice (optional)	
2 teaspoons toasted sesame oil	
mizuna leaves (Japanese mustard greens), to garnish	
Wakame Gomasio, to garnish	P.60

Place the bean curd strands in a heatproof bowl, cover with boiling water and soak for 1 hour, until rehydrated.

Rinse and drain the bean curd strands. Cut into 3 cm (1¼ in) lengths and add to the simmering vegan broth.

To assemble the ramen, quickly and evenly divide the warm drained noodles between two bowls. Pour the hot broth over, along with the bean curd strands. Add the zucchini, corn, kimchi and kimchi juice, if using. Drizzle with the sesame oil, garnish with mizuna leaves and wakame gomasio and serve straight away.

(NOTE) Bean curd strands are also called bean curd sticks. You'll find them in most Asian supermarkets.

87

醤油
ラーメン

You get the best of both worlds in this fusion bowl that combines two beloved Japanese staples: gyoza and ramen. The gyozas are crispy and juicy, the chashu pork melts in your mouth, and the noodles are firm yet springy, creating a total textural adventure. Warning: you'll be dreaming of this one tonight.

Shoyu Ramen

Seafood Gyoza and Chashu Ramen

Serves 2

6 slices Chashu Pork	P.46
800 ml (27 fl oz) Shoyu Broth, simmering	P.25
2 portions Ramen Noodles, cooked al dente and drained	P.37
20 g (¾ oz) fresh wood ear mushrooms	
8 pieces menma	
60 g (2 oz) leek, white part only, julienned	
1 Ajitsuke Tamago, halved	P.44
1 tablespoon finely chopped chives	
Black Garlic Oil, for drizzling (optional)	P.45
6 cooked Seafood Gyozas	P.53

Warm the chashu slices in the simmering shoyu broth.

To assemble the ramen, quickly and evenly divide the warm drained noodles between two bowls and pour the hot shoyu broth over, along with the chashu slices. Add the mushrooms, menma, leek and ajitsuke tamago. Top with the chives and drizzle with a little black garlic oil, if using. Serve with the seafood gyozas on the side.

89

醤油
ラーメン

Warm, nourishing and soul-reviving, this magical mushroom ramen might be the health remedy you've been searching for. Mushrooms have been a staple in Japanese cuisine for centuries, often used to recreate the umami depth typically associated with meat. Here, a medley of shiitake, enoki, wood ear, king brown and shimeji mushrooms builds a rich, layered broth that will have you slurping up every last drop.

Shoyu Ramen

Mushroom Ramen

Serves 2

25 g (1 oz) butter or oil	
1 teaspoon toasted sesame oil	
2 garlic cloves, chopped	
2 spring onions (scallions), sliced	
400 g (14 oz) mixed mushrooms, such as shiitake, enoki, wood ear, king brown and shimeji, sliced	
2 portions Ramen Noodles, cooked al dente and drained	P.37
800 ml (27 fl oz) Vegan Broth, simmering	P.31
1 nori sheet, cut into quarters	
1 tablespoon toasted sesame seeds	
½ teaspoon lemon zest	
Umami Mushroom Powder, to garnish	P.45

Heat the butter and sesame oil in a wok over medium–high heat and sauté the garlic until fragrant. Add the spring onion and mushroom and sauté for a further 2–3 minutes, until golden brown.

To assemble the ramen, quickly and evenly divide the warm drained noodles between two bowls and pour the hot vegan broth over. Add the stir-fried mushroom mixture and nori. Sprinkle with the sesame seeds and lemon zest, garnish with mushroom powder and serve straight away.

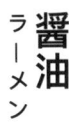
Dive into this surf-and-slurp sensation where crispy gyozas and juicy jumbo prawns bring a fresh coastal twist to the classic soy broth. The grilled prawns are a nod to Japan's obsession with flame-cooked seafood that finds expression in the island country's love for yakitori and robatayaki. Meanwhile, the prawn gyozas add a lighter, delicate flavour profile that completes the seafood soup.

Shoyu Ramen

Seafood Gyoza and Grilled Prawn Ramen

Serves 2

6 large raw prawns (shrimp), shells on	
1 teaspoon toasted sesame oil	
2 garlic cloves, finely grated	
2 teaspoons finely sliced red chilli	
2 portions Ramen Noodles, cooked al dente and drained	P.37
800 ml (27 fl oz) Shoyu Broth, simmering	P.25
6 cooked Seafood Gyozas	P.53
4 slices Narutomaki	P.57
2 teaspoons Furikake	P.61
½ teaspoon bonito flakes (katsuobushi)	
ponzu, for drizzling	

Place the prawns in a small bowl and combine with the oil, garlic and chilli.

Heat a chargrill pan over high heat and cook the prawns for 1 minute on each side, or until cooked through.

To assemble the ramen, quickly and evenly divide the warm drained noodles between two bowls and pour the hot shoyu broth over. Add the prawns, gyozas and narutomaki. Sprinkle with the furikake and bonito flakes and finish with a drizzle of ponzu.

At just a quarter of the size of standard chicken eggs, quail eggs have been a prized delicacy in Japanese cuisine for over a century. Soft-boiled and jammy, they add a creamy richness to this soy broth, with their petite size justifying a double serving. For a novel twist on the classic 'dippy eggs and soldiers', dunk your crispy gyozas into those bright, oozing yolks.

Shoyu Ramen

Kakuni, Vegetable Gyoza and Quail Egg Ramen

Serves 2

4 quail eggs	
6–8 pieces Kakuni	P.48
800 ml (27 fl oz) Shoyu Broth, simmering	P.25
2 portions Ramen Noodles, cooked al dente and drained	P.37
6 cooked Vegetable Gyozas	P.52
40 g (1½ oz) bean sprouts	
2 spring onions (scallions), finely sliced	
pickled ginger (beni shoga), to serve	
Pickled Shiitake Mushrooms, to serve	P.61

Bring a saucepan of water to the boil, add the quail eggs and cook for 2½ minutes. Cool in an ice bath for 3 minutes to stop the cooking process, then peel the eggs and cut in half.

Add the kakuni to the simmering shoyu broth to warm through.

To assemble the ramen, quickly and evenly divide the warm drained noodles between two bowls and pour the hot shoyu broth over, along with the kakuni. Add the gyozas, bean sprouts and spring onion and top with the quail eggs. Serve with pickled ginger and pickled mushrooms on the side.

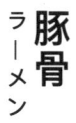

豚骨
ラーメン

A little bit naughty but oh-so-nice, this meaty ramen pairs crispy fried chicken with a fatty pork soup. Originating in the southern Japanese city of Fukuoka, tonkotsu ramen has an extremely rich, creamy broth made by simmering pork bones over the best part of a day. While the dish is traditionally topped with chashu, this modern take subs in chicken karaage – a stroke of pure genius.

Tonkotsu Ramen

Chicken Karaage Ramen

Serves 2

2 boneless chicken thighs, skin on, cut into 5 cm (2 in) pieces	
80 g (½ cup) potato starch	
¼ teaspoon sea salt	
¼ teaspoon freshly ground black pepper	
peanut oil, for deep-frying	
2 portions Ramen Noodles, cooked al dente and drained	P.37
800 ml (27 fl oz) Tonkotsu Broth, simmering	P.27
2 Ajitsuke Tamago, halved	P.44
2 spring onions (scallions), finely sliced	
2 teaspoons toasted sesame seeds	
Shichimi togarashi, to garnish (see note)	

Marinade

2 garlic cloves, finely grated
10 g (¼ oz) ginger, finely grated
1½ tablespoons soy sauce
1½ tablespoons sweet sake
1 teaspoon toasted sesame oil
¼ teaspoon ground white pepper
¼ teaspoon shichimi togarashi

Combine the marinade ingredients in a large bowl, add the chicken and mix well to coat. Cover with plastic wrap and refrigerate for 30 minutes.

Combine the potato starch, salt and pepper in a bowl.

Drain the chicken, discarding the marinade. Toss the chicken in the seasoned potato starch, coating it completely.

Heat enough peanut oil for deep-frying in a deep-fryer or large saucepan to 170°C (340°F). Fry the chicken in batches for 3 minutes, then transfer to wire racks to drain. Increase the oil temperature to 190°C (375°F) and fry the chicken again for 30–60 seconds, until golden brown and cooked through.

To assemble the ramen, quickly and evenly divide the warm drained noodles between two bowls and pour the hot tonkotsu broth over. Top with the ajitsuke tamago, spring onion and sesame seeds. Garnish with shichimi togarashi and serve with the chicken karaage on the side for dipping into the broth.

(NOTE) Shichimi togarashi is available from most Asian supermarkets.

We don't like to pick favourites, but this pork shoulder tonkotsu ramen easily ranks among Japan's greatest hits. To start, you've got the creamy, collagen-infused pork broth laced with umami goodness. Lean pork shoulder offers a lighter twist on the traditional chashu topping, while the onsen tamago add an irresistible creamy finish to bring it all home.

Tonkotsu Ramen

Pork Shoulder, Onsen Tamago and Narutomaki Ramen

Serves 2

1½ tablespoons dried wakame	
1 tablespoon Rendered Pork Fat	P.62
200 g (7 oz) Shredded Pork Shoulder	P.47
2 teaspoons soy sauce	
2 teaspoons mirin	
2 portions Ramen Noodles, cooked al dente and drained	P.37
800 ml (27 fl oz) Tonkotsu Broth, simmering	P.27
4 slices Narutomaki	P.57
2 spring onions (scallions), finely sliced	
2 teaspoons toasted black sesame seeds	
2 Onsen Tamago	P.44

Rinse the wakame and rehydrate in a bowl of cold water. Drain well.

Place the pork fat in a frying pan over medium–high heat, add the shredded pork and cook for 1–2 minutes. Toss the soy sauce and mirin through the pork and continue cooking until the pork is sticky and crisp.

To assemble the ramen, quickly and evenly divide the warm drained noodles between two bowls and pour the hot tonkotsu broth over. Top with the narutomaki, spring onion, wakame and shredded pork. Sprinkle with the sesame seeds and serve with the onsen tamago on the side.

101

豚骨
ラーメン

Salty, sweet, savoury, sour and just a touch bitter, this ramen hits all five basic flavour profiles. It also features three of Japan's most popular ramen toppings – chashu, ajitsuke tamago and menma – creating a bowl rich in both taste and texture. A drizzle of caramelised pork fat fortifies the broth, while black garlic oil rounds it all off with a smoky bitterness.

Tonkotsu Ramen

Chashu, Ajitsuke Tamago and Menma Ramen

Serves 2

6 slices Chashu Pork	P.46
2 teaspoons Rendered Pork Fat	P.62
2 portions Ramen Noodles, cooked al dente and drained	P.37
800 ml (27 fl oz) Tonkotsu Broth, simmering	P.27
20 g (¾ oz) fresh wood ear mushrooms, sliced	
8 pieces menma	
2 Ajitsuke Tamago, halved	P.44
1 nori sheet, cut into quarters	
Black Garlic Oil, for drizzling	P.45
2 teaspoons finely sliced garlic chives	
1 tablespoon Wakame Gomasio	P.60

Cook the chashu slices and pork fat in a large frying pan over medium heat until warm and melting.

To assemble the ramen, quickly and evenly divide the warm drained noodles between two bowls and pour the hot tonkotsu broth over. Top with the wood ear mushrooms, menma, ajitsuke tamago, nori pieces and chashu slices. Drizzle with a little black garlic oil and the remaining pork fat from the frying pan. Finish with a sprinkling of garlic chives and wakame gomasio.

103

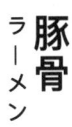

豚骨
ラーメン

Thick, chewy and packed with umami, king oyster mushrooms are the crowning glory of this rich tonkotsu ramen. Their mild earthy tones balance the fattiness of the pork broth, while adding a satisfying meaty depth. A drizzle of pork fat intensifies the flavour, adding an indulgent, velvety finish to every slurp.

Tonkotsu Ramen

Chashu Pork and King Oyster Mushroom Ramen

Serves 2

20 g (¾ oz) butter	
1 garlic clove, finely sliced	
100 g (3½ oz) king oyster mushrooms, sliced	
2 teaspoons soy sauce	
1 tablespoon Rendered Pork Fat	P.62
6 slices Chashu Pork	P.46
2 portions Ramen Noodles, cooked al dente and drained	P.37
800 ml (27 fl oz) Tonkotsu Broth, simmering	P.27
2 Ajitsuke Tamago, halved	P.44
1 carrot, julienned	
1 tablespoon chopped chives	
1 tablespoon warmed chashu braising liquid, for drizzling (optional)	P.46

Melt the butter in a wok or frying pan over medium–high heat. Add the garlic and mushrooms and season with sea salt and freshly ground black pepper. Cook, stirring, for 2–3 minutes. Add the soy sauce and cook for a further minute, until the mushrooms are golden brown, then remove the mushrooms from the pan and set aside.

Melt the pork fat in the same pan, add the chashu slices and warm through until meltingly tender.

To assemble the ramen, quickly and evenly divide the warm drained noodles between two bowls and pour the hot tonkotsu broth over. Add the mushrooms, chashu slices, ajitsuke tamago, carrot and chives. Drizzle with the remaining pork fat from the frying pan and the warmed chashu braising liquid, if using. Serve straight away.

105

豚骨
ラーメン

Just like a comforting bowl of bolognese, this ramen brings together al dente noodles and minced meat, stir-fried in a sweet and salty sauce. La doubanjiang – a spicy fermented bean paste from Sichuan – injects heat into the dish, cutting through the fatty tonkotsu broth, with chilli notes that linger just enough to keep you coming back for more.

Tonkotsu Ramen

Spicy Minced
Pork Ramen

Serves 2

1 tablespoon peanut oil	
300 g (10½ oz) minced (ground) pork	
¼ teaspoon ground white pepper	
1 tablespoon mirin	
1 tablespoon soy sauce	
1 tablespoon spicy chilli bean paste (la doubanjiang), or to taste (see notes)	
2 teaspoons caster (superfine) sugar	
2 teaspoons finely grated ginger	
1 spring onion (scallion), finely sliced	
2 portions Ramen Noodles, cooked al dente and drained	P.37
800 ml (27 fl oz) Tonkotsu Broth, simmering	P.27
6 cooked Pork Gyozas	P.53
10 green beans, finely sliced into rounds	
dried chilli threads, to garnish (see notes)	
2 Onsen Tamago	P.44

Heat the oil in a wok over medium–high heat and stir-fry the pork for 2–3 minutes, breaking up the meat with a wooden spoon. Add the pepper, mirin, soy sauce, chilli bean paste, sugar and ginger, then stir-fry for a further 1–2 minutes. Toss the spring onion through the mix, then remove the wok from the heat.

To assemble the ramen, quickly and evenly divide the warm drained noodles between two bowls and pour the hot tonkotsu broth over. Add the fried pork mixture and top with the pork gyozas and green beans. Garnish with dried chilli threads and serve with the onsen tamago on the side.

(NOTES) La doubanjiang can be purchased from most Asian supermarkets.

Dried chilli threads are also known as Korean chilli threads, *silgochu* or chilli strings. You'll find them in most Asian supermarkets.

豚骨 ラーメン

Life's too short to skimp on butter. Inspired by Hokkaido's butter corn ramen, this bowl features silky buttered cabbage that brings a subtle sweetness to balance the richness of the pork broth. With three layers of crunch – cabbage, kimchi and crispy pork gyozas – each bite is a flavour-packed textural delight.

Tonkotsu Ramen

Pork Gyoza and Buttered Cabbage Ramen

Serves 2

60 g (2 oz) shredded cabbage	
15 g (½ oz) butter	
2 portions Ramen Noodles, cooked al dente and drained	P.37
800 ml (27 fl oz) Tonkotsu Broth, simmering	P.27
8 cooked Pork Gyozas	P.53
100 g (3½ oz) Kimchi	P.58
1 tablespoon kimchi juice (optional)	
2 spring onions (scallions), finely sliced	
Black Garlic Oil, for drizzling	P.45

Bring a large saucepan of water to the boil over medium–high heat. Add the cabbage and blanch for 1–1½ minutes. Strain the cabbage, transfer it to a heatproof bowl, add the butter and toss to coat. Season with freshly ground black pepper.

To assemble the ramen, quickly and evenly divide the warm drained noodles between two bowls and pour the hot tonkotsu broth over. Add the cabbage, pork gyozas, kimchi, kimchi juice (if using), and spring onion. Drizzle with a little black garlic oil and serve straight away.

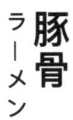

豚骨
ラーメン

If you're a fan of salt and pepper squid, you'll fall for this modern take on tonkotsu ramen. With roots in Sichuan and Cantonese cooking, salt and pepper tofu has become a popular vegetarian stand-in for shrimp or squid. In this bowl, crispy golden tofu cubes balance the rich pork broth with a mildly spicy crunch that's sure to win over even devoted meat eaters.

Tonkotsu Ramen

Salt and Pepper Tofu Ramen

Serves 2

2 portions Ramen Noodles, cooked al dente and drained	P.37
800 ml (27 fl oz) Tonkotsu Broth, simmering	P.27
50 g (1¾ oz) snow pea (mangetout) tendrils	
2 Ajitsuke Tamago, halved	P.44
2 teaspoons black sesame seeds	
black tahini, for drizzling (see note)	

Salt and Pepper Tofu

40 g (1½ oz) cornflour (corn starch)
3 teaspoons sea salt
½ teaspoon chilli flakes
1 teaspoon ground white pepper
1 teaspoon freshly ground black pepper
1 teaspoon toasted and ground Sichuan peppercorns
250 g (9 oz) firm tofu, drained, cut into 3 cm × 2.5 cm (1¼ in × 1 in) pieces
peanut oil, for deep-frying
1 teaspoon toasted sesame oil
3 red chillies, finely sliced
2 garlic cloves, finely grated
1 tablespoon finely grated ginger
1 spring onion (scallion), finely sliced
2 tablespoons soy sauce
1 tablespoon caster (superfine) sugar

To make the salt and pepper tofu, combine the cornflour, salt, chilli flakes, white and black pepper and ground Sichuan peppercorns in a large bowl. Add the tofu and toss to coat.

Heat enough oil for deep-frying in a deep-fryer, large saucepan or wok to 185°C (365°F). Working in batches, cook the tofu for 1–2 minutes, then transfer to a wire rack to drain.

Heat another 1 tablespoon peanut oil in a wok over medium–high heat and add the sesame oil, chilli and garlic. Cook, stirring, for 30–40 seconds, then add the ginger, spring onion, soy sauce and sugar. Cook for a further 30–40 seconds, then toss the tofu through to coat.

To assemble the ramen, quickly and evenly divide the warm drained noodles between two bowls and pour the hot tonkotsu broth over. Add the tofu, snow pea tendrils and adjitsuke tamago. Sprinkle with the sesame seeds, drizzle with a little black tahini and serve straight away.

(NOTE) Black tahini can be purchased from most Asian supermarkets or health-food stores.

ラーメン 塩

Adored for its light and mildly salty broth, shio ramen is all about letting the toppings shine. In this ramen bowl, pan-seared scallops add a touch of smokiness, while sweet bursts of corn brighten each bite. And that seaweed butter bomb? It's the secret weapon, melting into the broth for an extra creamy finish.

Shio Ramen

Seared Scallops, Buttered Corn and Leek Ramen

Serves 2

1 leek, white part only, sliced into 1 cm (½ in) rounds	
800 ml (27 fl oz) Shio Broth, simmering	P.29
2 tablespoons peanut oil	
12 scallops, with roe attached	
ground white pepper	
2 tablespoons melted butter	
2 portions Ramen Noodles, cooked al dente and drained	P.37
100 g (3½ oz) fresh corn kernels, blanched	
2 Seaweed Butter Bombs	P.63
dried chilli threads, to garnish (see note)	

Add the leeks to the simmering shio broth to cook through.

Heat the oil in a frying pan over medium–high heat. Season the scallops with sea salt and pepper, then cook, in batches, for 1–1½ minutes on one side. Flip them over, drizzle each scallop with a little melted butter and cook for a further 30–40 seconds, until golden brown.

To assemble the ramen, quickly and evenly divide the warm drained noodles between two bowls and pour the hot shio broth over, along with the leek. Add the scallops and corn, then top with the seaweed butter bombs. Garnish with chilli threads and serve straight away.

(NOTE) Dried chilli threads are also known as Korean chilli threads, *silgochu* or chilli strings. You'll find them in most Asian supermarkets.

Who doesn't love crispy chicken? This ramen bowl combines two of Japan's greatest comfort foods: golden, crumbed chicken and warm, soothing ramen. While shio is one of the oldest and simplest styles of ramen, the addition of panko-fried chicken is a 21st-century trend. Don't skip the tonkatsu sauce, which adds an irresistibly sweet tang.

Shio Ramen

Panko Chicken Ramen

Serves 2

2 × 150 g (5½ oz) boneless, skinless chicken breasts, pounded until 1 cm (½ in) thick	
50 g (⅓ cup) plain (all-purpose) flour	
1 egg	
60 g (1 cup) panko breadcrumbs	
peanut oil, for shallow-frying	
2 portions Ramen Noodles, cooked al dente and drained	P.37
800 ml (27 fl oz) Shio Broth, simmering	P.29
8 slices menma	
100 g (3½ oz) spinach, blanched and squeezed dry	
2 spring onions (scallions), finely sliced	
tonkatsu sauce, for drizzling (see note)	
2 Onsen Tamago	P.44

Season the chicken with sea salt and freshly ground black pepper. Place the flour in a shallow bowl, beat the egg in a second bowl and put the breadcrumbs into a third bowl. One at a time, dredge the chicken breasts in the flour and shake off the excess. Dip into the egg, then coat in the breadcrumbs.

Heat 3 cm (1¼ in) oil in a wok to 190°C (375°F). Fry the chicken for 2–3 minutes on each side, until golden brown and cooked through.

To assemble the ramen, quickly and evenly divide the warm drained noodles between two bowls and pour the hot shio broth over. Slice each chicken breast into 5–6 strips and arrange over the noodles. Top with the menma, spinach and spring onion. Finish with a drizzle of tonkatsu sauce and serve with the onsen tamago on the side.

(NOTE) Tonkatsu sauce can be purchased from most Asian supermarkets.

Get your daily greens all in one go from this wakame-powered shio ramen. Spinach, bok choy and edamame beans dance in the clear, salty broth, adding a vibrant pop of colour and a nutrient-packed crunch. The wakame not only infuses the broth with a subtle oceanic flavour but boosts your intake of iodine, calcium and iron. Talk about #healthgoals.

Shio Ramen

Spinach, Bok Choy and Edamame Ramen

Serves 2

1½ tablespoons dried wakame	
2 portions Ramen Noodles, cooked al dente and drained	P.37
800 ml (27 fl oz) Shio Broth, simmering	P.29
100 g (3½ oz) baby spinach, blanched and squeezed dry	
1 baby bok choy (pak choy), halved lengthways and blanched	
95 g (⅔ cup) edamame, blanched	
2 Ajitsuke Tamago, halved	P.44
3 teaspoons Wakame Gomasio	P.60
chopped garlic chives, to garnish	
toasted sesame oil, for drizzling	

Rinse the wakame and rehydrate in a bowl of cold water. Drain well.

To assemble the ramen, quickly and evenly divide the warm drained noodles between two bowls and pour the hot shio broth over. Add the wakame, blanched vegetables and ajitsuke tamago. Sprinkle with the wakame gomasio, garnish with garlic chives and finish with a drizzle of sesame oil.

Dark, decadent and daring, this ramen is what your midnight dreams are made of. The use of squid ink represents a new wave of ramen innovation in Japan's buzzing urban centres such as Tokyo. It gives the broth a striking black hue, while infusing it with a subtle, briny flavour that evokes memories of summer days spent by the sea.

Shio Ramen

Squid Ink Ramen

Serves 2

2 teaspoons peanut oil	
250 g (9 oz) squid tubes, cleaned and cut into 1 cm (½ in) thick rings	
2 teaspoons ponzu	
2 portions Ramen Noodles, cooked al dente and drained	P.37
2 teaspoons squid ink (see note)	
800 ml (27 fl oz) Shio Broth, simmering	P.29
4 slices Narutomaki	P.57
small handful of watercress	
3 teaspoons salmon roe	
toasted black sesame seeds, to garnish	

Heat the oil in a wok over medium–high heat. Add the squid and quickly stir-fry for about 1 minute, until opaque and just cooked through. Add the ponzu and toss to coat. Remove from the heat.

To assemble the ramen, quickly and evenly divide the warm drained noodles between two bowls. Quickly whisk the squid ink into the simmering shio broth, then pour over the noodles. Add the squid, narutomaki and watercress. Garnish with the salmon roe, freshly ground black pepper and sesame seeds and serve straight away.

(NOTE) Squid ink is available in sachets from gourmet food stores and delicatessens.

Old traditions meet new additions in this toppings-galore shio ramen. Swapping the classic soft-boiled ajitsuke tamago for a crispy fried egg, this bowl has a satisfying crunch that balances the tender pork belly and light broth. Go all out with the trimmings – including spring onion, menma, pickled mushrooms and chilli oil.

Shio Ramen

Kakuni, Fried Egg and Spring Onion Ramen

Serves 2

1 tablespoon chicken fat, Rendered Pork Fat or peanut oil	P.62
2 eggs	
2 portions Ramen Noodles, cooked al dente and drained	P.37
800 ml (27 fl oz) Shio Broth, simmering	P.29
8–10 pieces Kakuni	P.48
8 pieces menma	
2 spring onions (scallions), finely sliced	
red chilli, sliced, to garnish	
chilli oil, for drizzling (optional)	
Pickled Shiitake Mushrooms, to serve	P.61

Heat the fat or oil in a frying pan over medium–high heat. Crack in the eggs and fry until the bottoms and edges are crisp and the yolk is cooked to your liking.

To assemble the ramen, quickly and evenly divide the warm drained noodles between two bowls and pour the hot shio broth over. Add the kakuni, menma, spring onion and fried eggs. Garnish with sliced red chilli and drizzle on some chilli oil, if you like. Serve with pickled shiitake mushrooms on the side.

Umami is the name of the game in this plant-powered shio ramen. Shiitake mushrooms, nori, miso and mushroom powder team up to create an intense, savoury depth, while grilled Japanese pumpkin and fresh corn add a subtle touch of sweetness. Trust us: you'll find it hard not to slurp up every last drop.

Shio Ramen

Vegetable Gyoza, Kabocha and Shiitake Ramen

Serves 2

4 wedges kabocha (Japanese pumpkin/squash), each about 1 cm (½ in) thick	
2 teaspoons butter	
2 teaspoons toasted sesame oil	
4 fresh shiitake mushrooms, sliced	
1 spring onion (scallion), cut into 2 cm (¾ in) lengths	
1 garlic clove, finely grated	
1 teaspoon soy sauce	
2 portions Ramen Noodles, cooked al dente and drained	P.37
800 ml (27 fl oz) Shio Broth, simmering	P.29
6 cooked Vegetable Gyozas	P.52
1 nori sheet, cut into quarters	
100 g (3½ oz) fresh corn kernels, blanched	
2 Miso Butter Bombs	P.63
2 teaspoons toasted black sesame seeds	
Umami Mushroom Powder, to garnish	P.45

Heat a non-stick chargrill pan over high heat and grill the kabocha for 1–2 minutes on each side, until lightly charred and cooked through.

Place a wok over medium–high heat, add the butter and oil, then quickly toss the mushrooms, spring onion and garlic through. Cook for 1–2 minutes, add the soy sauce and toss to combine.

To assemble the ramen, quickly and evenly divide the warm drained noodles between two bowls and pour the hot shio broth over. Add the stir-fried mushroom mix, vegetable gyozas, nori, kabocha and corn. Dot the corn with the miso butter bombs and sprinkle with the sesame seeds. Garnish with a little umami mushroom powder and serve straight away.

Power up with this protein-packed noodle soup, featuring lightly fried chicken and silken tofu. A leaner substitute for fatty pork, the minced chicken is amped up with a spicy bean paste dressing made from six of Japan's staple condiments: pepper, mirin, sugar, soy sauce, chilli and ginger. It's the ultimate bowl for fuelling those gains.

Shio Ramen

Minced Chicken with Spicy Bean Paste Ramen

Serves 2

1 tablespoon peanut oil	
300 g (10½ oz) minced (ground) chicken	
¼ teaspoon ground white pepper	
1 tablespoon mirin	
1 tablespoon soy sauce	
1 tablespoon spicy chilli bean paste (la doubanjiang), or to taste (see notes)	
2 teaspoons caster (superfine) sugar	
2 teaspoons finely grated ginger	
1 spring onion (scallion), finely sliced	
2 portions Ramen Noodles, cooked al dente and drained	P.37
800 ml (27 fl oz) Shio Broth, simmering	P.29
120 g (4½ oz) silken tofu, cubed	
Black Garlic Oil, for drizzling	P.45
bean sprouts, to garnish	
dried chilli threads, to garnish (see notes)	

Heat the oil in a wok over medium–high heat. Add the chicken and stir-fry for 2–3 minutes, breaking up the meat with a wooden spoon. Add the pepper, mirin, soy sauce, chilli bean paste, sugar and ginger, then stir-fry for a further 1–2 minutes. Toss the spring onion through and set aside.

To assemble the ramen, quickly and evenly divide the warm drained noodles between two bowls and pour the hot shio broth over. Add the stir-fried chicken mixture and tofu. Drizzle with a little black garlic oil, garnish with bean sprouts and chilli threads and serve straight away.

(NOTES) La doubanjiang can be purchased from most Asian supermarkets.

Dried chilli threads are also known as Korean chilli threads, *silgochu* or chilli strings. You'll find them in most Asian supermarkets.

Published in 2025 by Smith Street Books
Naarm (Melbourne) | Australia
smithstreetbooks.com

Distributed outside of ANZ, North & Latin
America by Thames & Hudson Ltd.,
6–24 Britannia Street, London, WC1X 9JD
thamesandhudson.com

EU Authorised Representative: Interart S.A.R.L.
19 rue Charles Auray, 93500 Pantin, Paris, France
productsafety@thameshudson.co.uk;
www.interart.fr

ISBN: 978-1-9232-3914-2

Smith Street Books respectfully acknowledges the
Wurundjeri People of the Kulin Nation, who are the
Traditional Owners of the land on which we work, and
we pay our respects to their Elders past and present.

Note:
The recipes and text from this
book were previously published
in *Ramen-topia* (2017).

Publisher: Paul McNally
Art Direction and Design:
Evi-O.Studio | Evi O
Recipes, basics, essentials, toppings
and extras: Deborah Kaloper
Recipe introductions and additional text:
Melissa Woodley
Editor: Katri Hilden
Photographer: Daniel Herrmann-Zoll
Stylist: Deborah Kaloper
Home Economists: Caroline Griffiths
and Meryl Batlle
Production Manager: Aisling Coughlan

Printed & bound in China by
C&C Offset Printing Co., Ltd.

Book 390
10 9 8 7 6 5 4 3 2 1